Thank you Sir,

Lashawn Toney

LASHAWN M. TONEY

J.O.R.G.I.A.

Journey Of a Real Gift Inside Autism: From Beyond a Mother's Eyes

First published by Stellar Creative LLC 2022

First edition

ISBN 978-1-387-36726-9
Imprint: Lulu.com

Contents

Foreword

My name is LaShawn Toney. I am a mother of five amazing children. I married the love of my life, Gary Toney 23 years ago on March 20, 1999. We were together 3 years before we decided to tie the knot.

My husband and I always wanted a big family but after having Jorgia, at birth, getting the news she was diagnosed with Cystic Fibrosis devastated our family in ways you can't begin to imagine. Then 2 years later we were blindsided with her diagnosis of autism. Our family has definitely experienced things you wouldn't believe. My goal for telling our story is hoping to help other parents that may be struggling to understand autism, to let them know every feeling and emotion is valid, and they are not alone! How to use those feelings and know it's very important that we continue to fight for our children that need us to be their voice.

My hope is that after reading this book you will begin to understand my journey and know that with hard work and arming yourself with the right information you will begin to understand the real gifts that lie within autism. My daughter is my everything and I will advocate for her as long as I am breathing until our voices are heard loud and clear. When you are given a gift, you have to unwrap the gift to see and understand what it is. When you begin to unwrap autism and see and understand what it is, you will learn to love and cherish the gift you were given.

Thank you,

LaShawn M. Toney

Preface

The Meaning Behind The Title

Journey of a Real Gift Inside Autism

I wanted to explain the meaning behind the title and how it was given to me. Years ago I wanted to write this book realizing how many people I was helping along the way and wanted to reach even more people. I wanted to share my story to let parents that have children with autism or any disability for that matter know it's not easy, and it's definitely a challenge and will test your will and strength. I prayed that God would give me a title with meaning, a title that will hopefully capture people's attention. I also wanted to honor my daughter, who has been a true gift from God. Here is the day and the beginning of how this book emerged.

I was putting her to bed one night, and I was really trying to come up with a title for this book. As Jorgia lay there while I'm rubbing her back, a voice out of nowhere said call it JORGIA. I thought I was tripping, but I started saying Jorgia over and over. As I was saying her name I happened to look at her name that was above her bed on the wall and as I looked at each letter it's like God was giving me the words to say Journey Of a Real Gift Inside Autism which as you can see the first letter of each word spells out my daughter's name JORGIA. I ran downstairs screaming," I knew what to call my book", as my husband stared at me like I had lost my mind. I was so grateful to God for this magnificent title that says it all and honors my daughter beautifully. I of course added "Beyond a Mother's Eyes" because no one else can tell this story but me, through the eyes of Jorgia mom, emerged our story, our journey of fighting autism.

Acknowledgement

I would first like to thank my husband Gary Toney who has always encouraged me from day one to write this book. He has been there for me in more ways than I can count. He always believed in me and I love him more than ever, my best friend, the love of my life.

Thanks to my amazing kids Shana McClay, Shamari McClay, Garyn Toney and Garrion Toney for always pushing me to finish, reminding me how important it was to get this book done for all the other parents that are experiencing the same things. How important it was for Jorgia's voice to be heard.

Thanks to my friend Dee Neal for inspiring me to keep going and also giving me the connections I needed to make this all come together. Thanks to Katt for introducing me to Paula that made this all come together.

Thank you to my Aunt Joyce Henderson for her prayers that god would guide me on what I needed to say.

A special thanks to CARD for putting together an awesome team to help Jorgia in the areas she was struggling and helping me as a parent overcome some challenges I was having with her. You guys never gave up on us, and it's still a work in progress. CARD is definitely the best fit for my daughter, and I'm forever grateful for all the hard work and patience with my family.

Thank you to everyone, friends and family for all your words of encouragement. It has truly been a blessing to be able to tell my story and I could not have done it without all of you making me believe in myself.

I would like to thank Paula Lorraine, my publisher, for taking the time to talk to me when I needed her, answering all my questions to ease my mind as well as my husbands. Thank you for most of all taking on my story and being excited to publish it. Thanks to you, you made this whole process very easy and even more exciting. You are an amazing woman, and I'm so glad I was able to get to know you and can't wait to work together again.

A special thanks to Jorgia, this would not even be possible if it wasn't for you being you. Thank Jorgia for introducing us to autism. Thank you for just existing and being you!

Thank You

Dedication

I would like to dedicate this book to my sweet baby girl Jorgia. You may never read this or understand the love I have for you. I want you to know I see you, I hear you, through me your voice will forever shine through. I can't imagine everyday how you must feel not understanding the world through your eyes. Mom and dad will never leave you, we will remain right by your side until the day we are able to tell autism goodbye.

Your strength cannot be measured you are definitely one of a kind. Because of you babygirl I was able to face autism, and my reason for living I would find. God placed you in my arms and my life has never been the same. Everything about you has always had meaning, even within your name. Autism tried to break us, Autism tried to destroy everything we stood for, from autism came the best gift in the world and that I am sure.

You will always be the reason my heart beats, the reason I am who I am today. We will defeat autism one day at a time and nothing will stand in our way. We love you Jorgia through all the pain, through all the ups and downs. We will forever be grateful for your existence, and together we will take autism down. We will never give up on you; you're our special gift sent from heaven, like you, there will never be another. The beginning I admit was rough, but forever I will be honored to be your mother.

We Love you, Jorgia Danyelle Toney.

Love, Mom and Dad

J.O.R.G.I.A.

Chapter 1

I grew up in a family and a time when mental illness wasn't talked about much. It was only made known when you would see people with mental illness in public, at stores, or occasionally at schools. It was the unknown that scared me because I didn't understand it. Now that the tables have turned, I need my journey to be shared. I wanted to be heard, and parents with children suffering from any disability to know they are not alone. I'm not just writing a story; this is a real, life-changing journey through my eyes as Jorgia's mom. This is my story about dealing with a devastating diagnosis of autism, as well as another unexpected disease that changed our lives forever.

First, here is a little about me. I was born LaShawn Marie Brown on January 18, 1972, to my mother Barbara Ann Henderson. Walter Ray Brown was my dad, but he was never there for me, even when I was born. My mom was a single mother my whole life. She never found that one true love, but I had lots of aunts, uncles, and cousins in my life. My mother had seven sisters and four brothers, but strangely I was an only child. Of course, being the only child had its pros and cons. For the most part, I always wished I had a brother or sister. Even now as I think about it, with my mom working every day, it got pretty lonely sometimes. I would have loved to have siblings to talk to or confide in.

I never knew my father. As a matter of fact, I never met him. I spoke to him several times on the phone and exchanged pictures from time to time. I knew he was also an only child, but that's about it. A few years ago, I was notified that he had passed away. I never met him or that side of the family at all. Even though my mom had a big family, I seem to always feel alone, although I wrote poetry all the time to express myself. I guess being alone taught me to tap into the creative side of myself. I decided that whenever I had a child, I would make sure they had a brother or sister. Unfortunately, even though I had more than one child, life did not go the way I imagined. I truly understand the saying that life is unpredictable. I had it all planned and mapped out when I was about ten years old, but God definitely had another plan for my husband and me. If you had told me I would have been 47 years old with five children, one of them autistic and diagnosed with Cystic Fibrosis, I would have said you're crazy. Our family has been through some things you wouldn't believe.

This…is our story.

Chapter 2

To understand our story, I want to tell you a little bit about my family. When I met my husband, I already had two children from a previous marriage. Shana, my daughter at the time, was four, and my son Shamari was two. After I met my husband, we married three years later, on March 20th, 1999. Seven months later, on October 22nd, my son Garyn was born. On November 5th, 2006, my son Garrison was born. I knew we would have a big family. My husband came from a big family, unlike myself. I wanted my kids to always have one another if no one else. I was so happy living my life with my Prince Charming. He was the love of my life and my kids, and I adored him.

After Garrison was born, my husband and I yearned to have one more child. The kids were growing up so fast we wanted another baby in the house. We decided to try for a girl. On September 3, 2008, Jorgia was born. This is where life took a turn we would never forget. After having four children, you just know when something is not right. I started noticing unusual behavior with my daughter Jorgia not to mention she wasn't reaching developmental milestones like my other children. Jorgia seemed really unsociable and made very little eye contact. I remember this particular day when Jorgia was a toddler. I had her on my lap playing with her. She was smiling and laughing. I tried to stand her up on my lap, and her legs would just fold, every time. I knew at this age she should be pushing up a lot more, but she was just not there. This was the second time I had a gut feeling something was going on with her, so I eventually made a doctor's appointment to have her checked.

They said she was just a little delayed, but my gut told me there was more to it than that.

Before Jorgia was born, I dreamed of having a little girl. As a little girl, I played with dolls, believing that one day my dream would come true. Yes, I had a daughter from my previous marriage, and I was grateful, but back then I was young and in a toxic relationship. It was hard to enjoy my children or even realize what I had. I really wanted another opportunity, because I missed out on so much with my daughter Shana, whom I loved with all my heart. So, when I went for my ultrasound, and they told me it was a girl, I felt like I had just won the lottery. I couldn't believe God had just answered my prayers, and my dreams were really coming true. I was truly on top of the world. I couldn't wait to call and share the news with my husband and children. We were both so excited because it was something we both desired.

I had to have a scheduled C-Section, because I had one previously, so I was fine with it. We scheduled the surgery for September 3rd, 2008. The anticipation was killing us, waiting for this little princess to arrive. The months were passing so slowly because the excitement was so overwhelming. September 3rd finally arrived, and the procedure went as expected, with no complications. During the surgery, when the doctor asked me what I was going to name her, I said, Jorgia. The doctors began singing the song "Georgia," made famous by Ray Charles. She was named after my husband's mother, who passed away when he was only one month old, so her name meant a lot to us.

I very vividly remember the day Jorgia was born. I remember how it felt when they pulled her from my tired body and heard her soft cry. When they showed me my daughter, it was one of the happiest feelings of my life. She was perfect in every way; she was everything I had imagined and more. I held her so close all through the night. I didn't want to let her go or let her out of my sight. She was all mine.

The next morning, it was time for her feeding, and my motherly intuition bell started to ring. That was the first time I felt like something wasn't right. I noticed she seemed like she wasn't getting full during her feeding. I remember thinking a newborn shouldn't ever drink that much, but she just couldn't get enough. I ignored that little voice inside, thinking it wasn't much to worry about. At the time, I didn't know this was a sign of something I wasn't prepared for, that would be just the beginning of our lives never being the same.

We finally got to go home, and I was enjoying life with my family and my new baby girl. She was definitely the star in our house. About a week later, I got a phone call that would turn our lives upside down. I said "Hello" and the person told me they were calling from Valley Children's Hospital Pulmonology regarding Jorgia. I told them they must have mistakenly called about my son Garyn because he had been there before for asthma. The person said, "No ma'am, we are calling to inform you that your daughter's newborn screening tested positive for Cystic Fibrosis." I screamed, "Cystic fibrosis," What is that?" I asked, "Is she going to die?!" A million questions were running through my head and out of my mouth.

The nurse asked, "Have you spoken to her doctor? He was supposed to call you." I answered "No." then she told me she thought the doctor had already called and spoken to us. Since he hadn't called, she told me she could not disclose any more information or answer any additional questions until I spoke to my child's doctor. I hung up the phone in shock.

The feeling I had at that moment was almost indescribable. It was literally like electricity shooting down my entire body from head to toe. My heart was shattered. My head and chest were pounding. I felt as if I stumbled into the deepest, darkest hole and couldn't see anything but darkness. It literally brought me to my knees as my face was drenched in tears. The unknown was horrifying, and I felt like it was invading my life. I just couldn't believe it, I didn't want to believe it, and I wasn't ready to accept anything I had just heard. There was a harsh reality slapping us in the face. I couldn't help but wonder, "Is this all my fault? Was God punishing me for the abortion I had years ago?" I thought my world was perfect, but suddenly it seemed to be crumbling right before my eyes. I felt totally sick to my stomach. I even wondered if this was a dream. If so, I asked God to please wake me up from this nightmare. I couldn't stop crying long enough to even fill my lungs with the air I needed to let out any sound. I would have given anything including my life to take this disease away from my perfect little angel. My heart was crying, "Let me suffer God, let me take on this horrible diagnosis, not her. She didn't ask to be here." I felt all my strength draining from my body as it began to feel weaker and weaker. All this was happening in this one moment. I thought I was going to die, but I knew now I had to live for her. I knew we were in for the fight of our lives, and I didn't even know where to begin. I didn't even know what this was. I was mad at God because I thought he finally made a mistake. But, at the same time, I needed him now more than ever.

After trying to get over the initial shock, I phoned her doctor to set up an appointment to discuss this mysterious diagnosis, something I had never heard of in my life. After about a week of being in shock and the devastation of it all, my head was hurting from countless nights of crying and days of not eating. My husband and I went in to meet with the doctor. He informed us that she would have to go in for a CF (Cystic Fibrosis) sweat test to positively diagnose her, but from her screening he was sure she had Cystic Fibrosis. He told us it was a disease that attacks all her major organs (lungs, pancreas, intestines, etc.) He said people with CF have very thick mucus that they are not able to cough it up on their own. Eventually bacteria can grow in their lungs and causes an infection. They are also very susceptible to germs. When this occurs, she would need to be admitted to the hospital for a minimum of 16 days for what is called a tune-up. It requires round-the-clock breathing treatments to try and loosen the phlegm. If that doesn't work she would have to have a bronchoscopy, which is scraping of the lungs to remove that stubborn mucus that can sometimes get trapped in pockets of the lungs. The most terrifying news of all (as if this wasn't enough), was that there is no

CURE for the disease! The life expectancy when Jorgia was diagnosed was ten years old, but with all the research and technology, the age is now 38 years old.

I was completely and utterly sick during our consultation. I could hear what the doctor was saying, but sometimes I could see his lips moving, and there was no sound. My mind was racing, and our whole world that day was flipped inside out and upside down. It was never the same. I was sure God hated me somehow. I wanted to know, "Why God? Why me? Why her?" I just didn't understand. CF was also known as a white man's disease. It is one of the most common genetic disorders in white people in the United States, occurring in one of every 3,200 live births. It is less common in African Americans (1 in 17,000). My husband and I both carried the gene, so there was 1 in 5 chance that one of our children would inherit the disease, and Jorgia was our fifth child. I thought, "Oh my God, what have I done to my baby? I wish she was never born because she doesn't deserve this!" The odds were astounding. Little did we know, a diagnosis of Autism was still waiting right around the corner.

A few weeks later, we scheduled the sweat test, which was very simple. They put something like a blood pressure cuff around her arm and measured her sweat glands and other things I didn't quite understand. Later, they called and said the results were positive. I think deep down inside I already knew, but I was still shocked at what was happening. After weeks of trying to process this horrible news, I began doing some research to find out more about this disease, and what I needed to do to make sure my daughter lived a long, productive life. I didn't want this to stop her from whatever she wanted to do or be. I began to get her medications in order. I had to do an exercise with her to keep the phlegm loose, and this was done by hand. The exercise involved hitting her in certain areas on her body with a suction cup for 30 minutes for five to ten minutes at each site to keep her mucus thin and loose for three times a day every single day. When she got older, I received what's called a smart vest machine that she would have to use on a daily basis to help with this process. I didn't have to do it by hand any longer, because she was big enough to withstand the shaking of the machine. It's strapped on like a vest, and it shakes her at different speeds and levels. She didn't enjoy it at all, of course. She hated it. I hated it for her. While the vest was shaking her, I had to give her the breathing treatment simultaneously. The breathing treatments were done by what they called a Nebulizer. It came with all the tubing and cute little dinosaur mask I had to place over her nose and around her head to keep it on. My daughter was crying and shaking as smoke from the Nebulizer filled the room. My poor baby looked and sounded like a robot, because as she cried the vibrations from the vest would make her cry vibrate as well.

It was so hard to see my baby crying, not wanting to take her treatments. I was always smiling and telling her, "It's okay, mom is right here." I really wanted to shut the machine off and take it all away. This was killing me inside, but I had to do it because this was only to help her. Anything I needed to do to treat the disease and prevent flare-ups, I was all in 100 percent, whether I wanted to be or not. I prayed this would pay off in the long run.

In the meantime, I began to notice other things about Jorgia that just weren't sitting right with me. I know the doctor said she was just a little delayed, but I felt something else was really going on. I couldn't put my finger on it. I would notice her at about eight months old sitting and staring at the wall, rocking back and forth, and flapping her hands up and down. She also wasn't trying to crawl, she wasn't playing with toys, not responding very much, even when you called her name. I felt she just wasn't where she should be developmentally. As a mom you just know and have to follow your gut instincts.

I spoke to her doctor again and he finally had me call Central Valley Regional Center to schedule a psychological evaluation. The appointment was set, and I took her in. They tested her and evaluated her for about an hour, then told me they would contact me later with the results. The next day, I got a phone call saying she was just delayed and would eventually catch up, just to give it some time. There was nothing to worry about. I was confused and upset because I knew they were wrong. I just felt no one was listening and didn't understand. Jorgia was the one suffering, and as her mom, I knew she needed help. I knew I couldn't give up; I had a feeling they would be seeing me again.

I continued her CF treatments at home and kept a close eye on her. As time went on, I was still dealing with accepting the CF diagnosis. I was scared, and I was trying to grasp what had happened to our baby girl. Life was extremely different. I wasn't just a mom; I was a nurse and a care provider. It was all so overwhelming and very consuming but giving up was not an option. I was determined to fight for her in any way possible. A few months passed, and I spoke to several family members and friends who were concerned about Jorgia. I was also going back and forth with my husband regarding her delays and the abnormal behavior. They all basically convinced me to speak to her doctor again. At this time, Jorgia was almost 2 years old and still wasn't walking. She was crawling very little, army crawling most of the time. I finally decided to speak to her doctor, who suggested contacting the Regional Center again, requesting another psychological evaluation. I took his advice, called the Regional Center, and scheduled another evaluation. I was so nervous that the results would prove what I have felt for a while. I was hoping I was wrong, but I had a feeling I would be right. Being right wasn't always a good thing, especially in this case.

I waited on pins and needles for the appointment day to arrive. I was beyond anxious and so scared my stomach was hurting like I had been punched in the gut. I just didn't know what to expect. The day came very quickly, and when we arrived at the office, they immediately took us back to begin the evaluation. During the evaluation, we were taken from room to room to see if she could do little things like stack blocks, respond to certain noises, respond to certain commands, or if she would answer simple yes or no questions. It seemed like I was even asked a million questions. It was a very grueling process. After about an hour and a half, the test was complete. Jorgia and I both were exhausted from a long day, but I was glad it was over. We were told to await a phone call explaining the results of the evaluation.

The next day I got a call asking if I could come back in to speak to the psychologist. I had a feeling this wasn't going to be the answer I was hoping for, but the answer I already knew. I didn't know what to expect, I couldn't even sleep the night before. I laid awake thinking, "Where do I go from here?" I wondered what the psychologist would say. I just didn't sleep at all. My mind refused to shut down. I think as soon as I closed my eyes, it was already morning. I was beyond tired, but I was ready to finally get some long overdue answers. I just wanted to get Jorgia the help she needed, I wanted to do whatever they required me to do. I was upset, because if they found something wrong, that meant they missed it the first time, and she could have been treated sooner. Since she wasn't properly diagnosed, I felt the longer we waited, the worse her condition became.

Sitting in the waiting room at the Regional Center was tough. My stomach was in knots, I could actually hear my heart beating so hard and fast. I tried to stay calm for Jorgia because I didn't want her to feel how terrified I was. My name was called, and as I walked back to see the psychologist I felt the tears welling up in my eyes. I felt my legs turning into noodles, but I managed to keep putting one foot in front of the other. I reached his office and sat down. He started off by thanking me for not giving up on Jorgia, and for bringing her back. He also apologized and admitted they were wrong. He then began to go over her test. Once again I heard bits and pieces, but then I heard loud and clear as I held my breath... "JORGIA HAS AUTISM." I then felt all the air completely leave my body. I felt like I had just run a marathon. I thought I was going to pass out and I just kept thinking, "Are you kidding me God, what's next?" I was now angry, thinking this could have been detected earlier, but they got it wrong. Now the work and research were my first priority.

I was immediately surrounded by a familiar dark cloud. I didn't know what I was going to do. How was I going to break the news to my husband? Would the kids understand; would they still love her? So much was going on inside my brain at that moment. What the doctor said to me after that is unknown. I knew the answer a long time ago, but now it was confirmed. I was hoping I made the right decision taking her back for testing. I was sure I was right, but now there was another unknown, dark path I had to travel, and I wasn't ready. I probably will never be ready. I was determined to do everything I could for Jorgia, my heart was in pain for my baby. It seemed like bad news was always waiting for us at every turn on this journey. I was ready to take a detour if I only knew it would lead to a better path, but I wasn't willing to take that chance. There wasn't even a detour option available. I had to stay on this path and face this autism demon. I needed all my strength and the hand of God to help me stay on this journey and fight, but I didn't want to fight alone. Autism was bigger than me, but I had to be stronger. The only way to stand up to this was to equip myself with as much information as possible. It was going to be a never-ending road, but I was going to do everything in my power to sustain. I had to stay focused on what was important to break through this powerful obstacle.

I was assigned a Regional Center caseworker for my daughter. She would be very important along this journey. The goal was to try to get Jorgia started with early intervention therapy. She was also there to recommend other services to support me as her parent and caregiver, and also share any programs I wasn't aware of.

When I arrived home, my heart was heavy; knowing I had to sit down with my husband Gary to tell him the news I had just received. As I was crying, I just kept saying, "I'm sorry, I'm so sorry." He asked why I was saying I was sorry. I told him I was sorry I couldn't give him the perfect little girl we both desired. I felt like I had failed him. My job was to deliver a perfectly healthy baby girl, and I couldn't even get that right. I hated myself for that. I looked my husband in his eyes as the tears began to fall. I managed to get the words out to tell him Jorgia had Autism. He was surprised and shocked at the news, as his heart was broken and hurting for Jorgia. He was devastated for his baby girl, his princess, the one who he wanted to give the world on a silver platter.

He then told me he will never stop loving Jorgia, and there was nothing to be sorry for. He said, "We are her parents, and we will do whatever we have to do to give her whatever she needs. We will learn as much as possible about this monster they call Autism." We were determined to be prepared for what was coming. He also said, "Jorgia is perfect. Our perfect little girl." He refused to see her any other way, and I quickly agreed. I felt a bit relieved and totally understood every word he said, it was all absolutely true.

Chapter 3

I never questioned his love or mine for Jorgia. I knew I loved her more than anything, and I knew I would have to fight like crazy. Basically, I had to fight like I never had before. I would say I was absolutely petrified for what was ahead, but even that was an understatement. My heart was just in pieces for my princess because she didn't deserve this. Being a mom, I always want to make everything better, but it was out of my control. Not being in control was hard to accept. Mothers are supposed to make your pain go away, soothe you when you cry, kiss your boo boos, and everything would always feel better…but this. I could never make it better, and it was literally killing me.

The crazy part about this is when I was growing up, I would see kids on those little yellow buses. I had no clue what their experience was or what it was like for their parents for that matter. As a child, of course, we laughed at those kids because we didn't understand. Now realizing my daughter may be one of those kids on the little yellow bus, and that was nothing to laugh at. I now understood and was motivated to teach my kids that a disability is nothing to make fun of or laugh about. A disability meant they were special and needed our support. They couldn't help that they had a disability, and we had to learn to have empathy and understanding. We had to change people's perspectives one person at a time. I can't change the past, but I can damn sure start with my family.

Jorgia not only had a dual diagnosis of autism and Cystic Fibrosis, but she was developing patchy spots on her skin that looked familiar to me. I already knew exactly what it was. Both my sons and I had psoriasis. I lived with psoriasis my whole life, from a little girl up until now. It was such a horrible thing to live with, because of how visible it was on the skin. I was made fun of in school and bullied because kids didn't understand what I had. They thought it was contagious, so their reactions were very cruel, once again because of the unknown. *There is no cure for psoriasis.* Unfortunately, this phrase seemed to haunt my family over and over. My sons were also diagnosed at an early age, so when I saw the patches on her skin, I wasn't surprised. She was scratching continuously until she would bleed. I knew she was uncomfortable. I took her to the dermatologist, who confirmed what I already knew. They started her on Humira injections that I had to give her every other week, as if I needed one more thing added to my list. These injections had to be alternated between her stomach and right and left thigh area. I was worn out, I felt totally empty. I had to derail my focus back to what was more important at this time, now that I had better control of the psoriasis. I had so much to learn, there was still so much left to unravel.

I didn't know a lot about Autism, but I had a lot to find out. Jorgia was approaching two-years-old very quickly, and I still hadn't even heard her little voice. She would barely try to walk. I would have given my right leg just to hear her say mama or even daddy. I just wondered and waited to hear what her little voice sounded like. The little things in life we take for granted, those things never really mattered before, but now it was all I thought about. It taught me to better appreciate more of the things in my life, especially the little things. I took for granted giving birth to a healthy child. We don't realize how blessed we are for each one that is healthy, because you never know when something like my situation can make you see life through a whole new set of eyes. I will never look at things the same. Jorgia has changed my whole perspective on life.

My research began, wanting to learn as much as I could, talking to doctors, researching on the internet 24/7 non-stop. It became consuming. It was all about my princess. I wanted to know what it was like to be her; she was truly in her own little world. I would look into those big, beautiful eyes, and I would start to cry, because I knew she was in there dying to come out. I knew that her little girly personality wanted to shine. I knew she had a lot to say, and I wanted to hear every word. I literally prayed for that day to come. I needed her just as much as she needed me.

During my internet research, I ran across a quote that has stuck with me to this day. It said:

"Imagine you were in a foreign, noisy, and crowded city at night, not understanding the language spoken, recognizing only a few words but not really comprehending situations taking place around you, wanting to express a need for help but not being able. This experience may begin to help you relate to what a child with AUTISM feels like on an ordinary day."

Of course, I began to cry again, holding my daughter ever so tightly. I wanted her to know I tried to understand how she felt, and I would always be there. She would never be alone. I was always on the internet. There were a lot of scary videos of kids with Autism. Her doctor would tell me to stay off the internet, but that was tough, because I just wanted to know everything possible. Autism has such a wide spectrum. I came across a book written by Holly Robinson Pete, an actress who wrote a book with her daughter about her brother with Autism. I followed their story, which was very inspiring. It was called, "My brother Charlie." I also learned that Tisha Campbell, also a well-known actress has a son with Autism, and I began following her story as well. These types of stories gave me hope and helped me keep fighting for Jorgia.

Eventually, a representative from Central Regional Center called saying someone would contact me to begin early intervention therapy for Jorgia. This early intervention would start to work with her on several things such as speech, playing with toys, being social, sounds, etc. I received the call, and they set a schedule to start coming out every day for three hours a day to our home so she could be in her own environment. I was excited to see how she would progress with the therapy. The therapy was good for her. I didn't see a lot of change, but she really enjoyed the attention. Sometimes the therapist would push her and cause her to become very upset. The therapist told me it might get worse before it got better, and worse it did get. They had to push her to see what she could and couldn't do. Just like any other kid, she would not want to do things she didn't like or didn't want to do. Anytime they required her to do something they knew Jorgia was able to do, she would refuse or get angry to avoid doing what was asked of her. According to the therapist, this was to be expected and they had to keep pushing her. If they stopped because she became upset it would only teach her how to get out of things she didn't want to do.

For me, therapy started to seem like such an invasion of privacy, but I totally understood it was for her, so I couldn't let my feelings get in the way. I just wasn't used to having people in my home constantly every day. They were in my kitchen, in my bathroom, in my living room, everywhere I turned there were people. It was definitely a change for our family. It took some time to accept it, but I never got used to it. Gary worked every day trying to support the family, so I had to hold down everything at home, not just with Jorgia, but with my other four children. It was very stressful, to say the least. All I could think about in the back of my mind was how all I wanted to do was have some fun with my princess to give us a mental break from all the madness. This was not what little girls her age was supposed to be doing. It wasn't fair! Not a day went by that I didn't cry, or my heart wasn't breaking piece by piece for my baby girl. I wanted to do something normal for a change. I remember my son Garrison asking me "Can't we just take her back to the store and buy another sister?" That statement broke me down. He loved his sister but even as a little boy he could feel my anxiety and stress. I think he was just sad for his mom. I had to keep pushing, not just for Jorgia but also for my other children who mattered just as much.

Chapter 4

I had heard about beauty pageants for little girls and thought that would be a great outlet for Jorgia. Perhaps it would be something that would give us that normalcy I was searching for. I started searching online for pageants in our area and ran across the California tropics Pageant for girls. I read up on it to find out the requirements to sign her up. Once I found out all I needed to know I registered Jorgia immediately. I was super excited and couldn't wait to get started. This is exactly what we needed; it was for sure what I needed to give me a change of pace from all the madness. The pageant was about an hour away in Visalia from Fresno and it was about a month away. I began to look for pageant dresses for Jorgia. I was enjoying all of it. I had dreams of this moment, and now I had a princess and now I was about to dress her up like one. I wanted everyone to see how beautiful she is.

My baby had Autism and I was trying my best not to let autism have her. I started getting her sponsors for the pageant and collecting donations to help pay for all her category entrees and her entree fee as well as her attire. This was going to be just what I needed to get my mind off of this crazy roller coaster we had been on the past two years. Right before the pageant Jorgia had finally begun taking steps trying to walk, which brought us joy to see her progressing in that way. I was truly overjoyed because I wasn't sure if that day would ever come. All my children before Jorgia definitely walked before two-years-old so this was a long wait but it sure was worth it.

The pageant day was vastly approaching, and Jorgia was also still going strong with therapy. I finally received her pageant dress in the mail. It was a gorgeous pink dress with white lace, white lace socks and beautiful matching pink bows for her hair. It was more than I had imagined. I wanted to cry when I saw how beautiful my princess was. She was absolutely a vision of beauty. I couldn't believe she was my daughter. I really couldn't wait now to show her off. After seeing her I was sure she would win.

The day arrived to leave for the pageant. I however was a little worried about how she would act being around that type of atmosphere and crowd as well as being on stage, but I had to try. I had to know if she would fit in or if people would notice something different about her. I wanted her to just have a normal day. We arrived at the Hilton Hotel in Visalia where the pageant was being held. Jorgia was in a great mood. I got her all dolled up and her dress fit so perfectly even with the pacifier hanging from her mouth. We walked in and there were little girls everywhere. They all looked like little princesses from head to toe. I was so nervous I was shaking. I just hoped she had a chance to at least place in the pageant. To me she was the most beautiful little girl in the entire room. No one in there matched up to her. If she didn't win I was ready to accept that because she had already won in my book. She would always be Number One.

We checked into the pageant and got her number to pin on her dress. Now we just had to wait to be called to go in front of the judges. She was doing very well so far, calmly sucking away on her pacifier. Within about 20 minutes they called her name to walk the stage and be presented in front of the judges. Since she had just learned to walk I had to walk on stage with her. Her hand gripped my fingers so tightly as she began walking slowly and sucking on her pink pacifier. Even though she was two, with her delay Jorgia was still like a baby. She still managed to walk the stage like a true princess but eventually I had to pick her up to show her to all of the judges. You could hear the crowd sighing and whispering how beautiful she was. People always talked about her eyes and how big and beautiful they were. How bold, big, and black her eyelashes were, so beautiful they looked unreal.

When I got back to my seat whether she won or not I was so proud of how well she did, she was always first place in my book. The awards ceremony started, I was trembling as I looked at my husband sitting in the audience like a proud father with his camera, taking every photo he possibly could. When they said first place beauty goes to "with a long pause "JORGIA TONEY. I couldn't believe my princess won, 1st place beauty, 1st place for best eyes, and 1st place for best hair and photogenic. She really was a princess now and forever. I was happier than I have been in a long time. I was so proud of her. It was the most amazing feeling to walk upon that stage and have her receive her crown and trophies. I couldn't wait to tell everyone I knew and display her awards proudly. I knew without a doubt we would do this again and I couldn't wait.

The next few years I continued doing a few pageants to have some sense of normalcy for her and me as well, but even the pageants got more difficult. I entered her into another pageant that had three categories: Beauty, Wow Wear, and the bathing suit competition. I thought in the back of my mind it might be a bit much for her, but I had to give it a shot. Once again, I began trying to find dresses and I also started going around the neighborhood collecting donations for her fees to enter the pageant. It was beyond exciting to get all these new cute little outfits that I knew she would look so beautiful in.

This time I actually rented her pageant dress because it was very expensive to purchase the dresses they required her to wear. I also purchased her Wow Wear from a girl I found online who custom made her outfit. It was a cowgirl theme, and her tutu skirt was made out of hot pink and black bandannas with matching bows and cowgirl boots. My husband and I built a float, ordered a life size horse, and attached it to the float we built. I then dressed the horse in the same outfit as her. We also attached a rope for her to pull the horse onto the stage. It was absolutely amazing and made me that much more excited. I was trying to win, I wanted to show them that autism didn't matter, we could be creative, and she could actually win. I then began searching for the perfect bathing suit outfit and I decided to go with the red, white, and blue American theme, again, with matching bows and flip flops. I had my son Garrison to be in this category with her acting as her lifeguard with the buoy, sitting in the background in a little lifeguard chair ready to save his sister. He was excited to do this with his sister. It was so much fun organizing this whole thing. It was also a lot of work, but I hoped it would all be worth it.

Pageant day arrived and it was held in Fresno at the Radisson Hotel Downtown. There were so many people and pure chaos. I was afraid that this might be too long of a day for Jorgia but there was no going back now. We hurried in and started to get her dressed for the first category which was Wow Wear. She looked like the most beautiful cowgirl I had ever laid eyes on. Everyone started heading to the stage where we waited to go on. Jorgia was doing well at the moment. She looked like she didn't know what was going on, but she was going with the flow for now.

We stepped up to the stage as my husband brought up the float. They asked what song I wanted her to walk in on. I chose Georgia Peaches by Lauren Alaina. This was more than perfect. The song came on and I grabbed her little hand and began walking slowly onto the stage with her float slowly following us and the crowd went wild. I heard everyone singing and clapping and I think I heard a couple of Yee Haws. Jorgia wasn't crying or smiling, she just had a blank look on her face, but it was the cutest thing you ever wanted to see. After we finished we hurried off stage to get ready for the Beauty category. I put her in this gorgeous black and pink lace beaded "bling-bling" dress that was a showstopper. She was absolutely stunning, I wanted to cry but I held it together as we again headed for the stage. Jorgia started to get a little fussy because it was already turning into a long day. I knew I was tired. I can imagine how she felt.

We went on stage again and she still had that blank look but now she started to whine, I think she had enough. I knew we had one more category to get through, but I started doubting if she would make it, she was exhausted and sleepy. I changed her quickly for the 3rd and final time. We got ready for the bathing suit competition. We went on stage, and she was crying on and off. Garrison looked confused; it was a hot but adorable mess. I wouldn't have changed anything. They managed to get onto the stage, and I started to walk her around showing off her bathing suit to the judges as Garrison sat in the background waiting to save his sister as we had rehearsed. When it was his turn he tried putting the buoy around her neck, but Jorgia wasn't having it. It was supposed to go all the way down to her waist to pull her off stage. Garrison wouldn't give up though. He only managed to get it around her neck and begin pulling her as I was trying to help him, scared he would choke her. I could hear the crowd laughing and clapping. It was the cutest thing, but it definitely didn't go the way I planned, but it was OK. They did a great job, and I was a proud mom. I'm sure the audience got the picture.

Now the awards are about to be handed out. I was so nervous I couldn't stop sweating and I think I was hyperventilating. Jorgia had fallen asleep on my shoulder which was better than her crying. She was exhausted so I let her sleep. The first award they called was the Beauty category. When they got ready to announce the 3rd place winner, I held my breath as I thought to myself, "I don't want 3rd place but I'll take it." The announcer leaned into the microphone and said "Jorgia Toney." I didn't move because I wasn't sure I heard it correctly. My husband nudged me and said, "Babe it's Jorgia! You gotta go on stage!" I was like Oh my God! Everyone was clapping. I went up on that stage with Jorgia still sound asleep on my shoulder. She had no clue of what was going on. I was a little disappointed but yet so proud.

We finally got to the Wow Wear category and again, they started to announce 3rd place. I think my heart literally stopped. I remember thinking, "She better not place 3rd again because this whole place was jumping when she was on stage." They didn't call her name. I didn't know if I was happy or scared. Now 2nd place was getting ready to be announced. I dropped my head with my hands over my face hoping she would be called if not 2nd possibly 1st. They still didn't call her name for 2nd either. At this point my stomach started hurting, I was so afraid she didn't place at all. I was in shock that she didn't win. I couldn't believe all that hard work and it didn't pay off. I was ready to leave and was starting to get upset when all of a sudden I heard 1st place Wow Wear winner Jorgia Toney echoing through the room! My mouth dropped, I felt stupid for not believing in my daughter or myself. We deserved this award, and I was over the moon!

This was a moment I would never forget. I couldn't get on stage fast enough. Of course, she slept during the whole ordeal, but I was honored as her mom to receive these awards on her behalf. I was smiling from ear to ear. I stood there on stage looking out into the audience as my husband was clapping and smiling like a proud father. I remember thinking, "We did it and no one even knows she has autism." Sad to say she didn't place in the bathing suit category, but that's OK I think we did a fantastic job, and I was overwhelmed with emotions of happiness.

Since we had such a great experience we tried to keep competing in pageants, trying to duplicate that win again. It all became too much for Jorgia and she would just cry. The pageant days were too long, lots of changing in and out outfits, lots of people running around, and the waiting process was not good. It was very exhausting for her and the family as well. She wouldn't cooperate and it made it very miserable for all of us. However, she would win or place in every pageant, and at the end of it all Jorgia ended up with 20 Trophies, 19 crowns, a few metals and 3 plaques. One of her pageants we competed in later she won cover girl and was on the front of the pageant programs that day. When I walked in and saw her picture on the programs my heart melted. It had definitely been a wonderful experience for us considering what we were going through behind closed doors. With all that was going on it made it hard to continue.

Chapter 5

Every time the pageants ended, and we had to head home, and it quickly hit me like a ton of bricks that it was back to reality. When we returned home, without hesitation I proudly displayed Jorgia's crowns, trophies, and metals upon the shelf for everyone to see. What also struck me is that she didn't even know she won those pageants and more importantly she didn't even know how proud of her I really was and always will be.

She literally had no communication skills. Jorgia had her own way of communicating since she couldn't speak. When she wanted something she would grab my hand and throw it in a certain direction or towards what she wanted. I always had to try and figure out what she was asking for. If I didn't figure it out fast enough she would have a tantrum. Trying to understand her was very difficult and very frustrating at times. She would lose her pacifier or drop it somewhere and she didn't know how to tell me.

It would trigger a full-blown tantrum, because we had no idea what she wanted, or what she was trying to tell us. I had to put myself in her shoes to understand her. As she got older the tantrums became extremely unbearable. The most heartbreaking part was I could never do anything to help her process how she was feeling.

She would try to hurt herself by biting, scratching, pinching, and hitting herself, sometimes banging her head as well as trying to harm others. I just wanted to hold her ever so tightly and let her know I'm here and will always be here. If there was some way I could take the pain or whatever she was feeling away and put it within myself It would have been done in a heartbeat! I hated seeing her tantrum, I hated seeing her like this, because I knew she was trying to communicate something somehow. As tears were streaming down my face as I watched Jorgia throw herself all over the floor, hearing her gut-wrenching screams, I somehow felt I had failed as a mother. I never thought I could feel so helpless. I just didn't know what to do and those words were hard to accept. "God, please help me." was my new constant prayer.

Since it was hard for Jorgia to express herself or communicate, it frustrated her to where she would have very violent episodes and outbursts. The therapy did a lot for Jorgia, but the older she got she knew what she wanted and since we couldn't understand her it sent her into these horrible rages. These tantrums would happen at least five or six times a day. Sometimes I would have to try and hold her to keep her from harming herself but in the midst of it all she would literally turn on me trying to beat me up. I was hurt because I was only trying to help her and love her but at the same time trying to understand why she would want to hurt me. I'm her mother. A part of understanding autism is that the person with the diagnosis don't understand why they are doing the things they are doing. They are just trying to communicate how they feel whether it is frustrating or confusing to them they are overwhelmed with the unknown. I had to quickly learn to stop taking it personally; she just wasn't aware of how she was hurting me. These tantrums got worse as time went on and the older she got the stronger she became.

Jorgia got really attached to a little stuffed animal called Pablo from the cartoon The Backyardigans. She loves that little penguin. She had to take it everywhere she went. One day we were home and she wanted it, but we couldn't find it anywhere, of course I knew what was coming if I didn't find it. Sometimes it would be in the oddest places you wouldn't think to look.

The tantrum came shortly after we couldn't find it.

That stuffed animal was definitely her security blanket, her little friend. It's almost like she felt safe as long as Pablo was by her side.

When he was nowhere to be found she would get so angry. She would cry and scream until we were able to locate where he was. She had the whole house running around frantically trying to find Pablo. When we did finally find it, it was like we won the championship, screaming "We got it! We got It!" jumping up and down happily that we found it for her. Now that I look back it's hilarious but in those moments it was very critical. This was still all so new to me I was learning as I went, and it was the toughest thing I had ever been through in my life. After she comes out of her tantrums she would act like nothing happened and start playing and laughing. In the meantime, my body was hurting from being so beat up, I was physically and mentally drained daily, I felt like I just played a full game of tackle football. I knew why she would tantrum, but I just couldn't understand why she was trying to hurt me all the time.

The look in her eyes was dark and mysterious. It was like I could see her, but she wasn't there. It was like someone had taken over her body and she transformed into a whole other person. It was so unreal, I had never seen anything like this before, I was so scared and numb. Sometimes I would look at her in her eyes as my eyes filled with water whispering to her that I know she is in there and I always wondered what she was thinking or feeling. This has fully taken over my life. Even at home it was very difficult to have parties or friends over.

One of my most embarrassing moments was when we invited some friends over during football season to watch a Chicago Bear game because we were Bear fans. We were all sitting around watching the game, yelling, and laughing just having a good time. Jorgia was sitting on the couch next to my friend. Next thing I know my friend screamed like she had gotten stabbed or something, it was definitely a hurt scream. I looked over there and Jorgia had leaned over and bit her on the arm, her arm was very bruised, no broken skin but black and blue. I was so embarrassed and felt so bad my daughter had done this. All I could do was apologize over and over again.

One thing with Autism is Jorgia was also becoming very territorial. She didn't want anyone sitting next to me or talking to me especially if I'm on the phone. It was very hard for me to enjoy anything because I always had to keep an eye on her, other kids as well as adults. I was always afraid of her harming someone really bad, especially a child. I honestly felt like I had lost myself, I just couldn't be me because it now was all about Jorgia. She would attack at any time for no reason; we had to always be on guard. The tantrums were so horrific at times I wanted to give up, but I knew she needed me and in a strange way I needed her too. I couldn't give up. I was definitely motivated to take on Autism and not let it take over me. It became an ongoing challenge that I was drastically losing but was determined to keep going even when I didn't want to.

When she was about 3 years old her therapy team helped me get her off the pacifier, it was definitely a fight I thought would never happen but after many tantrums, crying and attacking me she finally stopped asking for it. I think at night was probably the worst because she wanted it the most to help her fall asleep of course. Jorgia was also still in diapers. I knew potty training probably wouldn't happen for a very long time, all that mattered to me was hearing her talk or communicate better. She still was my princess and I loved her more than life itself. I just had to figure out what I needed to do to help her evolve.

Besides therapy I also got Jorgia into speech therapy as well as occupational therapy with all these things going on. It was pushing her to do things she didn't want to do or didn't feel comfortable doing so naturally the tantrums became more and more aggressive, intense, and frequent. Early intervention was only up to 3 years old, so she then started therapy with BIA which were behavioral Intervention. It consisted of her own team of 4 girls that came to the house every day for about four hours working with her on communication skills mostly, playing games with her also being more self-sufficient. The hardest part about all this was they would tell me no matter what, don't interfere because it was going to get worse before it got better. I had heard this before and I knew what was coming but I agreed not knowing that this would by far be one of the hardest things I ever had to do. Every time she would go into one of her rages, they would just put pillows around her so she wouldn't bump her head and they would stand and watch her to make sure she would not hurt herself. As a mom I wanted to grab her, hold her, hug her, I tried to do anything to make her feel better or to let her know I was there, but I had to stay back and let them do their job. Sometimes I would just go in my room and grab a pillow and scream into the pillow as loud as I could, I would cry and pray asking God to give me strength, asking him to work a miracle, to please help her, help me to help her. Some days I felt like I was going to lose it.

I think the best thing from this therapy was when I heard Jorgia's little voice for the first time. I think I cried the whole day. She was starting to say "mom" or "Da-da," very small words, but I literally thought I would never hear her speak because she would just sit there, and she just wouldn't even try to make sounds. When I heard her say mom, it was the most beautiful thing I ever heard in my life. I didn't know whether to laugh, cry, jump or scream. I just know I felt it was such a huge accomplishment. It once reminded me of those little simple things we took for granted. This was not small to me. I was ready to celebrate. With Jorgia everything mattered.

Talk about being exhausted and emotionally drained dealing with Jorgia therapies on top of all my other kids in the home that needed their mom. I had turned into not only a mom and wife, but a nurse and a care-provider. I started to always feel tired, my body felt beat up and I was always in pain. I always felt like I was drowning and there was no way out. Even though I was married, even at times I felt alone. I often felt like I was neglecting my sons because all my time had focused on Jorgia. This was so unfair to them, but I was doing the best I could and hoped they understood. No one could ever understand what I was going through. Honestly, I felt at times I wanted to take my own life. I felt like there was no way I could go through this for the rest of my life. I felt like a prisoner in my own home.

Chapter 6

When Jorgia was born I stopped living and started surviving, Surviving CF and Autism had become my new normal. Starting to always feel so mad, sad, helpless, suicidal, feeling extremely depressed I thought it was time to seek out a support group. I needed to find out if there were people like me that felt like me. I am embarrassed to even admit I felt angry at times too at my daughter for being the way she was knowing it wasn't her fault. I did find a support group I absolutely loved. It was called Parents Unlimited where I met other mothers with similar issues that understood how I felt and didn't judge me. We talked, we cried, we shared stories after stories. It was definitely something I needed at that time and meeting new people that I became friends with was special to me. People say they understand what you go through, but they the parents in the support group really did understand.

I started to experience that feeling of losing myself and so afraid of the future with Jorgia because there was so much to learn and so much ahead we didn't even know about. I loved to work outside the home. It gave me opportunities to not only meet new people but to get away from it all and experience something different. I loved singing but I couldn't become a singer. I loved decorating, like home decorating or parties/wedding type events ever since I was younger. I absolutely loved writing poetry. All these things came to a complete halt after having Jorgia. I always felt I was living in a dark fog. Working outside the home just wasn't something I would be able to do, because I would come home and have to deal with overwhelming issues with her tantrums, and not sleeping very well. I never got to really travel or go see places I had never been before because traveling with her wasn't always a good idea. It was so much you had to take and remember to bring for her comfort ability it became not worth it to even go.

We traveled some but not much like family trips to Disneyland and Magic Mountain, places like that were OK but still a lot of work. Jorgia also wasn't a good eater at the time because of her cystic fibrosis. She was super picky and smelled everything before tasting. Sometimes she wouldn't even taste. The doctors had put her on ensure milk to give her body any nutrition she might have been missing. CVRC was such a blessing her worker made sure I was in every program that covered her milk and diapers.

Eventually I had to give up working and become a home care provider for Jorgia she needed me 24/7. There were nights she hardly slept or was getting up early. Her Primary doctor put her on several meds that just didn't seem to always work. We tried different meds which was very frightening. Jorgia was in and out of the hospital a lot.

We spent so much time at Valley Medical Center they practically knew us. I started to recognize certain signs of her getting sick. It took me a little while to learn her symptoms because she was not verbal at all and showed hardly any emotion. This was so exhausting trying to watch her every move and worrying with every cry or scream. Was she hurt? Was she in any pain? Was she scared? Was she nervous? I was constantly questioning her every movement or sound. Relaxing was a Joke. I became totally consumed because I love her so much and was praying for a miracle. In the back of my mind, I still thought somehow she would one day wake up and be normal. I knew God would answer my prayers but after several years I figured either God was still angry with me or I deserved everything that was happening to me, I thought I was cursed.

Jorgia's hospital stay became an experience I wouldn't wish on my worst enemy. Writing about it even now brings tears to my eyes. My princess is stronger than I ever could have imagined. This would have broken anyone down. I was just there supporting her, and she was the one helping me to be stronger. Even though there were multiple experiences with her being in the hospital there is one in particular that sticks in my mind because it was so horrific to see your child go through. I remember being at my son's garrison T-Ball game. Jorgia was probably about 3 years old, and one of the signs I was able to recognize was with Jorgia, who was already pretty quiet and to herself, but she would seem more tired, wanting to lay down. Her eyes would seem a little glossed over, and she just seemed not there. She also was already a picky eater which meant she only ate certain things that became her favorites. She didn't want those things at all. Her Apple Juice, chips, French Fries etc....

My son's game was almost over so I decided to just take her to the car and wait for my husband and my son. I strapped her in the car seat and proceeded to the front seat. I was sitting there for about 5 minutes, and I started to hear her coughing and gagging. I jumped back out of my seat. My heart was beating so fast I could hear it, by the time I opened the door she had vomited all over herself and the car. I was literally shaking. She seemed so lifeless. I jumped back on the dirt road where I saw my husband and son, I began to wave my arms profusely to get their attention to move quickly. My husband saw me and noticed I seemed to be in a panic and started to run towards us as fast as they could. We rushed her to the hospital. I lost count of how many times she vomited on the way there.

The problem was waiting in ER, these waiting rooms would always seem overcrowded which was always a horrible experience because you not only have a sick child with CF but an Autistic child that can become very impatient. I knew she was getting worse, so I called her Pulmonology Doctor from the waiting room through the after hours line and was able to speak with her. When I told her what was going on she said Jorgia needed to get back ASAP! She got a hold of the ER and within minutes they were calling us back. Jorgia wouldn't hold anything down; she didn't even have enough Strength to hold her head up. She kept looking at me with those big deep dark beautiful eyes like she was saying mama help me do something. Little did she know I was fighting with every being in my body to help her but never felt so helpless at that moment.

The doctor finally came in after several hours of torture with running test, her crying, moaning, and vomiting, and he said we have to admit her that the test came back showing her Pancreas was so inflamed which is due to the Cystic Fibrosis. This disease was attacking her Pancreas. The doctor said this is known as Pancreatitis which is very painful and the only way to get rid of it is nothing can go into the belly for several days or at least until her numbers come down. My heart dropped. How was I going to manage this? My poor baby can't eat? Normal readings where around 60 to 100 her numbers were reading about 1200. I was stunned. I began to make arrangements with my husband to bring me items I needed for her and her favorite things because I knew we would be there for a while. Now because of the phlegm that was starting to form Jorgia began to cough. She was getting worse by every passing minute. I never left her side, I was tired, hungry, scared, and feeling so bad for her. My

knees felt as if they wanted to give out from standing so long at her bedside to catch whatever was coming out of her, to rub her little belly to comfort her in any way I could. I couldn't afford to sit down.

The adrenaline was running so high at this point. The nurse came into the room to run an IV and this is where things got even worse. Jorgia not only had small veins, but they rolled. The nightmare began trying to get this IV going because she was so dehydrated from all the vomiting on top of it all. I would have never guessed getting an IV started would be an unforgettable experience. They poked my baby so many times her arms started to turn Black and blue. I was begging them to please stop, she had had enough. Asking them to please find the best of the best in this hospital for my baby's sake.

Her screams from the constant poking and prodding were so unbearable. About another hour passed and they found someone they labeled as the best. I prayed they were right. This nurse tried a few times herself, sad to say after several attempts there was still no success. My head dropped trying to hide the fact my eyes were watering up because I just wanted to scream and cry at the same time. My baby girl at this point had been stuck about 10 times. I didn't know if I was heartbroken or angry. Maybe I was both, along with a cluster of other feelings. I understood it was needed, but damn when is it enough! They suggested giving her a break because her room was ready. We were taken up stairs to her private room where she still continued to vomit, with no IV still in place. Jorgia and I sat in the middle of that room with towels underneath us where at this point she was dry heaving and starting to spit up blood and bright green bile. I was no longer holding back the tears. I was crying, my body felt as if I had been in a boxing match, my hands were aching, and my fingers didn't want to bend anymore. They were extremely stiff from holding on to her lifeless body for so long. I knew I had to keep pushing for her. I knew I was overwhelmed and exhausted, but I couldn't fathom how she was feeling. That's what mattered.

I was crying out where are you Lord please don't make her suffer because you're angry with me God. Please help my baby. Hopping God somehow heard me and would possibly work a miracle. I glanced at the clock on the wall and now it's probably about 10 pm. My husband and kids are calling with worry in their voices. wanting an update on their sister and my husband wanting to know what's going on with his princess. They were not happy with what I had to tell them but understood. My husband was also concerned about how I was holding up and offered to trade places with me and I of course declined the offer. There was absolutely no way in hell I was leaving my daughter. How I felt didn't matter. I was here to stay. I knew I had to be here for her, be her voice, watch over her because she wasn't able to speak for herself. I wanted to be her everything. I trusted my husband, but I needed to hear and know everything that was going on for myself.

The door to her room opened now they are rolling in an ultrasound machine to try and put this IV in by watching it on a monitor. I thought I was going to pass out. I could feel the rage building ever so slowly. Now we have about 5 to 6 people in there to hold her down so she can insert this IV hopefully to finally get something going to help her feel better. Jorgia was exhausted and sick. She didn't even move as they poked and poked and poked, tears streaming down my cheeks as I rubbed her little head singing a soft tune of her favorite nursery rhyme in her ear "Twinkle, twinkle, little star." I sang so gently trying to keep her calm and also let her know mom is still right here. Probably about 20 minutes later the lady said the words I have waited 4 hours to hear that seemed like 4 years, "I got it, it's in" she said. All I could say over and over was "Thank you Jesus, thank you Jesus." I felt God must have finally heard me. I was hoping this would start everything moving in a more positive direction. She was still having small episodes here and there. I definitely couldn't relax yet because my poor baby was still dry heaving blood and that bright green bile. Between episodes she would try to rest, but it was so difficult for her. She was just so sick.

During one of her resting periods, just in case I had to move quickly I was sitting in a fold up chair next to her bed watching TV, I happened to glance over at her checking to see if she was okay and what I saw made my head literally feel like it was spinning. I immediately became dizzy and nauseous because I had a feeling what was about to happen next. Jorgia's arm where the IV was from her elbow to her fingertips was blown up so tight, her hand looked like the shape of a baseball. I screamed "OH NOOO!" and began pressing the panic button as the light flashed red and the dreadful sound like a horn from an old model car rang out. To me the sound in my head was more like a fire alarm, waiting for the nurses to storm in seemed like it was ten minutes, but it was probably two to three seconds. I was about to give up, this night never seemed to get better, and it felt like the longest night in my life with no end in sight.

Whatever could happen was going to happen. I really honestly have never felt so weak in my entire life. I didn't know how I was going to make it through the rest of tonight, but I knew at the same time I just couldn't leave her. The nurses rushed in saying her vein must have rolled and the fluid was going directly into her arm, so they had to get the bandages off and remove the IV, and the words I dreaded hearing… "We will have to get another IV in." Now the rage was starting to boil, I lost count 15 times trying to get this IV started and it still wasn't over. When I heard her say they would have to do it again, I could barely stand. It felt like someone was pouring cool water on top of my head. Slowly, it flowed down my body, and I began to feel numb as it passed through every inch of my body down to my toes. I couldn't move. I wanted to just run and scream, but I couldn't move. I had to quickly snap out of it because my Jorgia needed me. My lips were trembling trying to hold it together. I was trying not to let her see me like that, I was trying to be strong for her. The nurses began to remove the bandages and tape they had on her arm and hand to keep the IV in place.

As they began to unwrap the tape and bandages my baby girl's skin began to come off with it. It was swollen so tight from all the fluid going into her arm, her skin was stuck to the tape. I was about to vomit. I was so angry that she was going through this hell. I felt my knees starting to buckle. My stomach was in knots, my head was pounding like I immediately got a migraine. My ankles were so swollen from standing all day, when I walked it felt as if my ankles wanted to burst. My feet where throbbing so bad It felt like if I moved my legs to walk my feet wouldn't follow. My baby was crying because she was literally being tortured. I just couldn't believe this was happening.

I laid my head down on her tiny little chest to hug her and hold her, as I kissed her cheeks and forehead telling her "It's going to be okay, mom is right here." I asked myself, what kind of mother am I that I couldn't do anything to help her feel better. How could I allow them to do this to her? Should I have stopped them? Should I have just left? Should I have just said NO? Now all these questions are clogging my brain. I felt like I had truly failed. I have never felt this level of helplessness in my entire life.

The team proceeded to come in and wheel JORGIA into another room where they turned off the lights to try and find her veins using flashlights under her arms, checking her feet or anywhere they could possibly put an IV. I was astounded by what was transpiring. Once again they poked, and poked, and poked. My baby wasn't crying anymore or moving. She had just given up. I felt a lump come into my throat that I couldn't swallow. I think the part of my heart that was broken was trying to come out. I would have given anything to trade places with her.

Her little body was so tired she just didn't have the strength to fight anymore. They still were unable to find her vein because of the extreme dehydration. They took her back to her room and within 15 minutes the doctor came in to inform me that she needed this IV immediately so they will have to unfortunately put it in her neck. I think I totally shut down. I lost my sense of hearing completely. Everything he said after that sounded like mumbles, but I was nodding OK even though I didn't hear anything he said. I wanted to grab my daughter and run for the nearest exit.

I tried to stay in the room as they prepped to put this IV in her neck. Before they started they said they needed her to cry so the vein could pop out making it easier to put in. When they said that I went into the hallway as my legs started trembling. I felt my stomach trying to come up through my mouth, and I could still see into the room as they began to hold her down. Understanding that Jorgia is considered non-verbal, she began screaming and crying saying, "ALL DONE! ALL DONE!" over and over. That literally broke me down right there in the hallway. I fell to my knees sobbing profusely. My body felt like I was just in a horrible car accident and my heart was bleeding. My heart literally hurt so bad I had to grab my chest and I could feel the palpitations throbbing against my fist like a stick beating a drum.

As I was in a ball on the floor I quickly called my aunt Joyce to pray on the phone with me because I was losing my strength, my patience, and not to mention my mind. I needed God in that moment to give me the strength I needed to get through the rest of this horrifying night. My aunt began to pray, crying out to God for mercy as I held the phone tightly to my ears crying uncontrollably. I was swaying back and forth, holding on to every word in that prayer, still on my knees as I could still hear my princess screaming.

After the prayer I gathered myself. When I saw the doctor approaching from Jorgia's room, I was wiping my face and fixing my clothes after what looked like I came straight out of a street brawl. The doctor said the IV was a success, and Jorgia was resting. I thanked him with malice still in my heart for hurting my baby girl even though I knew they were just trying to help her. I couldn't wait to see her. I rushed into the room forgetting every feeling my body was experiencing. Just laying eyes on her knowing she was safe made all the pain worth it.

The clock was now reading roughly about 2 to 3 am. After this long night I could say she was finally resting. Knowing the sunrise was due to come up soon I struggled to try and get a few hours of sleep in. There was so much on my mind and what we had just been though it was still so fresh. I could still feel a pain in my heart that wouldn't subside. With morning quickly approaching I think I must have dozed off but was awakened a few hours later with a team and a plan to get my daughter well and back home. I knew it would be a long journey, but I never left her side. After about 23 pokes and an IV in her neck, several days with no eating or drinking, believe me we still had some rough moments but it definitely made me stronger for everything that was still ahead of us. Jorgia was back home doing well about a week later.

Chapter 7

Jorgia was in and out of the hospital more than I could count because of her Cystic Fibrosis. I have spent three wedding anniversaries in the hospital, Easter in the hospital, New Year's in the hospital, and we have missed many holidays due to her hospital stays. We would go through the poking and prodding so much it just became mind boggling. Every time she would stay in the hospital I never left her side. I was there every minute, every day, every hour, which allowed me opportunities to discuss concerns like her being poked a million times. On top of that, waiting in the waiting room with Jorgia at the hospital or appointments was intolerable. I told the doctor I wasn't leaving this hospital until a plan was in place to prevent her being poked so many times. We just couldn't do it anymore.

The doctor agreed and explained to me there was an option to have a meta port put into her chest the size of a nickel just beneath the skin that will allow them to access IV's and blood draws. All together it will prevent her from having to be poked again. The downside to it he explained further would be having a nurse come out once a month to flush it to prevent blood clots. The flush will consist of the nurse inserting a needle into the port on her chest which is still a little painful, but it will require only one poke instead of 20. The last downside to this is she will require surgery to insert the meta port. Hearing all of this was very scary but yet gratifying knowing she would never have to experience what she has experienced the last few years. I agreed to schedule to have the procedure done.

The procedure was very simple however my nerves were a wreck, but I knew having this done would make our lives so much easier. That was the only thought that gave me a sense of peace. The day of the procedure my stomach was so queasy, I was just a mess. Nevertheless, the doctors and nurses were so reassuring and explained everything that would happen from beginning to the end. They made it very bearable and were so grateful, considering what we had already been through. She came through the procedure a little groggy which wore off quickly and she went back to herself in no time. Hopefully, this was the road to better hospital experiences.

Probably about two years after the port was put in, Jorgia never got sick to the point of being put in the hospital. I didn't know whether I felt upset or happy because I agreed to the surgery to prepare Jorgia for the next hospital stay that never came. Nevertheless, I was so thankful that she didn't have to go through that experience, and she wasn't getting sick. She still has the port flushed every month, but it was for nothing because she was doing so well with her cystic Fibrosis. I was not complaining, for once she was getting a break from the hospital.

After careful consideration and talking it over with my husband we decided to go ahead and have the meta port removed. There was just no reason to keep it in at this point. I made the call and got Jorgia scheduled. Her Mediport was removed after two years of basically getting flushed but not having to actually access it for an IV. We did access it a few times for blood draws which was great, so we were able to save her from the pain of being poked from that aspect. Unbelievably about two weeks later just after having the port removed, Jorgia started getting sick. I was confused. The moment I thought we were catching a break the rug was pulled right from under us. I felt as if someone punched me in my stomach and I was gasping for air. I just couldn't understand what the hell was going on and why God was allowing this to happen to my baby. Here we are after all that surgery and hard work to protect her from the very thing that was about to happen again, the IV situation.

She did end up back in the hospital again. The poking began trying to locate her veins to start an IV. I felt like I was in a twilight zone. I was trying to process why we were back here again and never got to use the damn Mediport. I was beyond angry and just wanted them to get this IV going as soon as possible. I could not withstand another episode like her last hospital stay. I know it had been a while, but the memory was fresh. They did try several times to get the IV in and shockingly they did get it probably on the 10th try. Which was still too much for me when you're watching your baby lying there screaming and crying because they are poking the hell out of her and she's not feeling well on top of that. She was suffering from pancreatitis again; it was very inflamed. Her numbers were high but not as high as they were the last time thank God. She was still in pain and once again had to keep her belly empty. That meant nothing to eat or drink for a couple of days. Letting the stomach rest helps the inflammation to go down.

She was admitted for a couple of days. We became a familiar face to the nurses and doctors. They knew I did not play when it came to my daughter. I wanted to know who her nurse was, what they were doing, and why they were doing it. Yes, I was that parent. I had to be. My daughter didn't have a voice, but I was going to make sure she would still be heard. They brought in a small refrigerator for me to store my food, blankets, and pillows. They knew I was not leaving. If she was here for a couple of days then so was I. After a few stays in this hospital, I must admit there were a few confrontations with some nurses over constantly waking her up all through the night after she would just get to sleep, after finally calming her down from snatching out IV's and throwing tantrums. I asked them why would you want to wake a child with autism after seeing what she can do? They replied they need to do vitals on her. I told them, "Those vitals can wait until morning and I'm requesting no one to come into this room the rest of the night." They kept waking up the beast then left me to tame her. It was unfair. Now that we were there in the hospital again, I didn't even have to request anything. They put the note outside the door that said, "Do not disturb until morning." That was awesome. I felt heard for once.

My husband and boys came to visit us the next morning. Jorgia was still not feeling well and was crying and whining. My husband picked her up and laid her head on his shoulder and began to pat her and rub her back to comfort her. All of a sudden he let out a sound I had never heard before, at the same time he lifted Jorgia up and she was latched onto his shoulder. She had bit him. His first instinct was not a good choice. He yanked her off and pulled a plug right out of his shoulder. He calmly laid her back down and left the room. I was stunned.

Jorgia is like that unpredictable snake you can't get too close to. It was hard to trust her, you just never knew what her next move would be, and she moved very quickly. She looked sweet and innocent, but she would attack soon as you let your guard down and relaxed. You wanted to hug her, kiss her, and comfort her but you just never knew what mood she was in or how she was feeling. I was her mom, and I was even scared to get close sometimes. When I did have to get close I went in very cautiously, I know what she's capable of so I tried to predict what she would do but I didn't always get it right. There were times I did get bit as well. Sometimes slapped or kicked.

The only good thing that came from this hospital stay for me was within those two years, to my surprise my other issue of having autistic kids wait for appointments or ER was addressed. I'm not sure how it transpired, but I was elated to find out about the new George's Law "not named after my daughter" It's actually named after George the Giraffe which is the hospital mascot. This Law, which is now in place at Valley Children's Hospital, allows parents with autistic children to be seen in ER or a doctor's appointments at priority level. They are allowed to be seen before other non-life-threatening patients to avoid the waiting that can lead to blow ups or tantrums. I knew all too well that waiting could become very uncomfortable for patients that are waiting and parents dealing with these children. It can also be scary for other children witnessing these actions because they don't understand what's happening. What's also exciting is they have also built sensory waiting rooms and areas for children like Jorgia.

This was huge progress for our autism community. It was definitely a step in the right direction, but we still have so far to go. I knew I not only had to be Jorgia's voice, but I wanted to help other parents with autistic children. When I was doing my research, there was not a lot of information out there. Now, knowing how little information I started with and knowing it wasn't easy gave me compassion for other families with autistic children. Everything helps and everyone matters. I want to share any and everything I found out or come across that could help make life easier in any way. I found out there were mobile blood draws that come to your home, so you won't have to bring your disabled or autistic child to the waiting room. I also discovered autism passes at amusement parks such as Disneyland or Magic Mountain which allow an autistic child and their party to go in front of the lines. I have gathered so much valuable information and have already begin helping others and can't wait to help many more.

Chapter 8

We continued with early intervention until Jorgia was about 4 years old where she started BIA services which they would still come to home but it was with a different company. Honestly, it just didn't seem to be working for me, but I kept going thinking she really needed this. I was not happy with the inconsistency from the therapist. It had a very high turnover rate which was very difficult. Jorgia would cling to a therapist, or a therapist would work so well with her and then she would quit or move up to a higher position. I was very happy for their promotions, but I was frustrated at the same time because that meant all the best therapists move on. Sometimes it would just be the girls calling in canceling sessions a lot. This became totally overwhelming because with an autistic child you know the number 1 thing I feel is they don't like change; routine is very important.

As time went on over the next few years I watched and monitored Jorgia with her therapist, some things I liked and some things I didn't. I did notice as she got older she was clinging to me more and more which hindered her learning and participation. At that time, I had to make a choice to try and get her therapy out of the home and into a facility. This would not only become a difficult transition for her but also for me. I wanted to watch her every move, I wanted to make sure she was being treated right "it was very hard to trust," but I knew her not being around me would allow her to pay more attention and help her grasp what she was being taught rather than worry about where I was or what I was doing. We started to have a few sessions outside the home at a school-like setting that was part of a church probably about 2 to 3 times a week and the other sessions at home. I didn't realize leaving her would be so hard. Sometimes I waited in the parking lot or outside the door. I guess I also didn't want to miss any progress or anything she did positively. I wanted her to know I was proud of any progress she made, but I knew I needed to do this for her.

People would tell me to go home or use that time as a break, but it really was easier said than done. This was my baby that couldn't speak for herself or was unable to tell me if anyone had hurt her or even if she was in pain. How could I relax? The most I did was go grab a cup of coffee. Eventually after so much inconsistency and taking her to this creepy place in the back of a church I started looking for another place willing to work with her. I found out about another place called CARD which stood for "Center for Autism and Related Disorders", and I heard great things about this center, and I was excited to see what they had to offer Jorgia. I called to see if they were accepting new kids and they said yes but of course we had to see if her insurance would cover her therapy. The process began. I was constantly on the phone checking to see If I could get approval for her as soon as possible.

While waiting for that call I received a different phone call that my son Garyn had passed out in the parking lot after football practice at school and had to be rushed to the hospital. My husband and I were already out and about and headed straight to the hospital after I hung up. While waiting as they drew blood and ran a test I was on the phone still fighting with the insurance to cover her therapy so Jorgia could start her sessions at CARD. After fighting for a day or 2 they finally approved it, and everything was a go.

I was super excited. CARD called me to come in for a tour and interview basically to discuss Jorgia and her needs so they can put together the best team for her. I got such great vibes from this place. They really cared and loved the kids here. They didn't treat them like they had a disability. The team would talk to Jorgia as if she understood them. I didn't get it then, but

I get it now. We might think because children with autism are non-verbal they don't understand. They are very smart and understand more than we think. We have to stop underestimating these amazing kids.

Jorgia did shock me sometime at the things she knew I didn't realize she knew. Especially since working with CARD they have been so loving and caring to Jorgia and she loves being there, she loves going, she absolutely feels very comfortable at the center it's almost like her second home. Some of her sessions are at home but that's OK because they are very respectful of our space as a family. Jorgia actually cries when she can't go due to her being sick or a cancellation. I think sometimes she would rather be there than home.

Jorgia has one special person that stole her heart at the center from day one, her therapist named Cindy. She calls her name everyday all day. No one knows why she repeats her name constantly, but she is definitely her favorite person. I love the fact that even though Cindy has been promoted she still makes time to spend with Jorgia. CARD is absolutely a dream place I recommend to anyone that needs a therapist for their child with autism or any developmental delays. They have even been there for me as her parent, and I am never left feeling out of the loop.

We have meetings constantly every week to discuss Jorgia progress and what else we can do to help her or things I want them to work on with her. They also kept in communication with her schools to make sure they were always all on the same page. That was very important to me and felt like I finally found the right place for my daughter. That cared about Jorgia in every way. I was being helped on dealing with her in the car or at home. It wouldn't always work but consistency is what I had to work on with myself. The more I stick to something the better it will become. CARD has been a

great fit for Jorgia and our family as a whole. My search was over and now it was about focusing more on Jorgia progress.

Chapter 9

When Jorgia was about five or six years old she was very needy and in constant need of attention. She was set on things she wanted and things she wanted to do. To avoid meltdowns, we tried to keep her happy by giving her whatever she wanted. Her neediness made it hard to take her places or take family trips or go on vacation. We did take some family trips from time to time and did a little traveling which was great, but bringing Jorgia became exhausting. Everything from packing all of her necessary items to keeping her happy and calm, to when she would tantrum or wanted something that wasn't available – all of it was a lot to keep up with.

Calming Jorgia down became a harder task than what I would expect. I learned through her therapy that we were feeding the bad behavior by giving her what she wanted when she wanted it. They taught me to make her ask, they worked with me on teaching her to wait, and also had her work for things she wanted instead of it just being given to her. Again, it got worse before it got better. Over time she showed signs of improvement but even now it's still something we continue to work on every day. We all had to break those bad habits of giving in to her. It was hard when you just wanted peace of mind, but we had to put in the work to be able to have that peace more often than just for that moment.

Jorgia was doing well with her Cystic Fibrosis. It had been a long time since she had flare ups. We had to be careful because she is very susceptible to germs that can make her very sick very quickly. I knew her birthday was coming up and wanted to do something special, I was a little scared of having a lot of people around that could potentially make her sick. I decided to give her a birthday party at Chuck Cheese. She loved going there. With my kids' helping we decorated the tables and chairs with pink, white, and purple balloons. All of her cousins, brothers, and sister were there. We were having an amazing time. However, the next day we suffered the consequences of having that party in a public place. My worst fears came true, Jorgia got very sick and ended up back in the hospital. I was so angry at myself for taking such a chance. I just wanted to treat her like the special princess she was. It was my fault, I felt absolutely horrible. Now she is the one having to go through this trauma again because of my carelessness.

The doctor said she must have picked up germs from Chuck E. Cheese that caused her to grow a bacteria that made her sick. It could have been something simple: a sick kid touching a surface that she ends up touching as well. This became one of the hardest things as a family not being able to do outings or take trips because we were always scared of her getting sick. We had to try and make the best of opportunities when we did go places. We tried to avoid becoming prisoners in our own home. I know it was feeling like that to me, but I didn't want that for my other children. I did my best to keep things as normal as possible for them. I never wanted Jorgia to interfere with me being the best mom to them that I could be. I'm sure I wasn't perfect, but I damn sure did my best for the circumstances I was enduring.

The good thing about taking her to Disneyland and places with special accommodations was the fact that everyone in our party was allowed to go in front of the lines. This was due to the fact that autistic children are unable to wait for long periods of time. It was still difficult thinking about her getting sick but most times we managed to keep her safe and it went fine. Being able to go in front of the lines made the trip less stressful, it definitely was a plus for family trips like this. Her tantrums at the time mainly consisted of screaming, crying, and trying to hurt herself. The older she would get the tantrums became more and more intense and aggressive, the things that used to calm her down were no longer working. This made traveling and taking trips more difficult to take.

It was hard as a mom wanting to be the best for all your children and trying to be there for all five was definitely getting harder to manage. It really hurt my heart when I had to say no we're not going or no we can't do something because of Jorgia. Jorgia's schedule on a daily basis was very hectic. She was not only in behavioral therapy, but she was also in occupational therapy, and speech therapy which eventually we had to stop because of her tantrums. They said it was really a waste of time. She was not fully getting what she needed out of the sessions because her behavior was getting in the way.

These tantrums seem like they worsened year after year. Jorgia started school which was hard for both of us. Knowing she couldn't communicate it made it difficult to leave her or trust anyone with her. I had to learn to let go and wanted her to feel my positivity and hope to make her feel safe. Inside I was struggling to leave her at school. I would be home pacing the floor, trying to stay busy, sometimes I would even call the class to check on her. I think I was making myself crazy, I was a nervous wreck. To my surprise she was doing very well. It is very true when they say, "A watched pot of water never boils." I watched that clock that never seemed to move waiting to pick my baby up every day. I couldn't wait to see her. Knowing she wouldn't be able to tell me how her day went, or if anyone did anything to her really worried me. It was to the point where I had to be really tuned into her needs. I was noticing every bump, bruise, scratch or even asking what she ate, or did she eat. Sometimes I felt the teachers were not understanding and seemed annoyed with me, but I felt it was my job to make sure they did their job and mine to protect my daughter who was incapable of protecting herself. I didn't care about how they felt. Having Jorgia has definitely brought out a side of me I didn't know existed. It was good in ways and sometimes it was bad. For example, there was an incident at a preschool she attended, which I was not happy about.

Upon visiting this school and taking a tour of the class she would be in I did not get good vibes about this teacher. It was something about her demeanor and her lack of excitement and compassion that just wasn't sitting right with me. She showed no type of emotion, and I felt some type of emotion was needed when working with children like Jorgia. I really didn't see that in her. She had worked there for years, which is the only thing that was making feel a little more comfortable. I shrugged it off trying to keep an open mind and give it a try. I continued with allowing Jorgia to attend the school. I packed her lunch every single day as well as took her to school and dropped her off every day. I was that mom. I had to make sure she was getting the nutrition she needed because she was a super picky eater due to her Cystic Fibrosis.

When I would pick her up every day I was very observant, which a parent should be. I would observe the other kids' behaviors such as kids banging their heads, screaming, crying, yelling, kids wearing helmets, kids put into areas where they couldn't leave. "Like a cage, but not a cage," it was very overwhelming. The teacher was almost emotionless, and nothing bothered her. The tone in her voice was monotone, her answers were always short, and she walked very slowly. It was almost like she was numb to it all. It took a lot to just make her smile. She just was very unapproachable or unlikable, but I was doing my best to understand. Maybe working with children like this took a lot out of her, but I also felt this was her career choice and if this was something she was no longer passionate about maybe it was time to retire. She was definitely beyond or at her retiring age.

I picked Jorgia up on this particular day as the class was walking down the sidewalk to the bus. As I was walking to my car, I proceeded to ask the teacher what Jorgia ate today so I could know how to address her eating once we returned home. The teacher answered "FOOD." That triggered something inside of me that I didn't know existed. Not only did I feel her answer was sarcastic but also disrespectful. There were tense words exchanged between us, mostly from me telling her how I felt about her bullshit answer! I told her that my daughter would no longer be attending her class.

I feel strongly that as parents of autistic children, we go through enough and don't need this level of treatment especially from a teacher who doesn't have to be there. We as parents don't have a choice of how our children are born, and we are doing our best with what we know and have. We expect a certain level of comfort and respect from our kids' teachers, and I felt she fell short of that by a mile.

I took my daughter home and the next few days I received calls from the school district and principal apologizing for the teacher's actions. I accepted their apologies, but I wasn't willing to bring my daughter back without an apology from the teacher herself and I felt a meeting had to be set. The school officials agreed and immediately scheduled the meeting. I went to the meeting and everyone attended including that teacher, the principal, and district superintendent and others. I can't recall their names or initial titles. I sat face to face with her because I wasn't intimidated. Apparently she was because she refused to give me any eye contact, which I thought was hilarious. If she was bold enough to give me that sarcastic answer then I felt she should be bold enough to look me in the eyes. I felt like I was in a bullfighting ring with my feet brushing the ground kicking up dust. All I saw was red, and I was ready to charge with horns down. I was angry, but at the same time I knew this was a big opportunity for me to speak my truth and hopefully make sure she understood how her actions affected me. Hopefully my actions would show other parents it's alright to speak up and stand up for yourself and your child because no one is too big or too high to make mistakes. I wanted to make a difference, so I had to be angry enough but also calm enough to get my point across that this was not acceptable. It seemed like such a small mistake and an easy fix, but it wasn't. It could seem small, but that's how it starts, and I wasn't going to let it get any further. It stopped right here with me.

The meeting started with the principal stating the facts of the incident and what transpired. Then the teacher began to speak saying how sorry she was with very little eye contact, and lack of emotion as usual. She stated that she didn't mean anything by what she said; she thought she was just answering a question. I felt that her apology was crappy, and I felt she didn't mean anything she said except the part when she was trying to make excuses for her actions. I began to tell her how I felt and what I took from her answer. I said the day I came in for the tour, and we met, we discussed many things regarding my daughter Jorgia and one concern I discussed with her was Jorgia's eating habits. I told the teacher at that time how I needed to keep up with Jorgia's eating, especially because of her Cystic Fibrosis and autism because she was extremely picky. Knowing this teacher was fully aware that I may ask about how her eating was for that day, when she answered "FOOD" I felt she was annoyed with the question and wanted to give me a quick answer to shut me up. I also stated to her that she had no idea what I go through as a parent of a child with a dual diagnosis. She didn't know what kind of day I was having and what I was feeling. To remotely think that kind of answer would be acceptable, she took a chance on thinking I had a good day. Good days are rare for me and that wasn't one of them. Even on a good day when it comes to my daughter I don't take that lightly. Good or bad day, that was not the answer I felt she should have given as a teacher to a parent that has voiced concerns about her child's eating habits or lack thereof.

I proceeded to tell them what I needed from the teacher in order for me to feel safe enough to bring my daughter back to her class. I needed her to chart daily what went in and out of Jorgia's mouth from the time I dropped her off until the time I picked her up. Maybe now she would think twice when answering a simple question. Furthermore, after that year my daughter would NOT be going back to that school. I was no longer comfortable and didn't feel an acceptable level of support from her as a teacher. I was proud of myself for standing up for what I thought was right. This was the first time, but it sure wasn't the last time I had to defend Jorgia or myself. Unfortunately, and sadly, everyone is not caring or empathetic to these types of situations or children with disabilities period. Jorgia attending school was often my worst fear.

Chapter 10

When Jorgia got to 1st, 2nd, 3rd grade it became a little easier. The teachers and teacher's aide she had at the school were phenomenal; and very different. They were caring, compassionate, understanding, and willing to do whatever they needed for Jorgia to be comfortable and for me to feel she was safe. They loved their jobs and it showed. Jorgia's tantrums really picked up in school. When she was in school she would try to hurt herself, other kids, and attack the teachers. She would try to pull their hair, she would try to hit them, she would totally disrupt the class. This was concerning for the teachers. Jorgia would scream, scratch, pitch and start to try and destroy property. I would get phone calls to pick her up, and when I would get to the class they would have her barricaded in the corner to keep everyone around her safe. The only one in this barricade who wasn't safe from Jorgia was herself. It really broke my heart because I knew she was trying to communicate something; I didn't know if something was wrong that she couldn't tell me. It was very hard trying to figure out what was causing her to become so angry. I remember there were times she would get upset or go into a tantrum just from hearing a baby cry or kids screaming. I don't think she liked hearing anyone in pain or distress. This happened a few times a week which made me worry even more. Her teachers were very good at informing me about her actions and what was going on. I was so appreciative that they did that for me.

When the weather would start to change, and it began to become very cold, Jorgia would have to miss school because of her cystic fibrosis. She would end up in the hospital for several weeks which would cause her to fall behind in school. When she got back she was confused because she hadn't been there for a while. It would really trigger her to start acting out having tantrums or meltdowns. Basically, every time she had to change her routine or things would be different she just didn't like it at all.

I remember Jorgia missing school for a couple of weeks because she started to get sick, which I tried to avoid by putting her coat on and putting a beanie cap on her head. I know people thought I was crazy or even teachers thought I was crazy and didn't understand why I was going to all this trouble when there was just a little bit of wind, or it was just a little chilly. Jorgia was a different type of child; she would get sick so fast that I had to protect her in any way I could. The beanie cap was to cover her ears to keep the air out and a jacket so she wouldn't be cold. Somehow, even then, sometimes that wasn't enough she will start to sniffle or sneeze. As soon as I heard that my heart would drop because I knew what was coming next. I was so tuned into Jorgia I could hear when she had a booger in her nose just by the way she was breathing. We could be sitting there just watching TV and I would ask my husband, "Do you hear that?", he would look at me like I was crazy and say, "Hear what?" I would say, "I think I need to suction Jorgia, it sounds like she has a booger stuck in her nose." I would go get the suction and start to suction her and what I was hearing would be quickly confirmed. He said he couldn't believe I heard that, shaking his head. I was just always on the edge listening for any sign of her getting sick.

It did not take very much for Jorgia to get sick. Thinking back on this particular time when she did get sick with Cystic Fibrosis, it was hard to cough up the phlegm. She would cough and cough, but it was such a weak cough that wouldn't come out. It was just trapped in her chest. Unfortunately, we ended up in the hospital and after about a week of breathing treatments and whatever else we could do to loosen the phlegm, nothing was working.

The doctor informed me that they would have to go in and do a bronchoscopy which is the scraping of her lungs to get the phlegm out that was stuck down in a pocket of her lungs. All I could do was hang my head shaking it in disbelief, but I knew it was the best thing for her and we were just exhausted and ready to go home. This was why I always dressed Jorgia as warm as possible during cold days or windy days.

My sons Garyn and Garrison were treated exactly the same way because of their asthma. I really was portrayed as the weird crazy mom with the kids that wore big jackets and beanie caps, but I was doing whatever I thought was best to keep my children safe. I just knew what being sick looked like in our home and I knew going to the hospital was turning into a routine. I was trying to avoid that at all costs. I didn't care what people thought, especially when they were not the ones taking care of my children.

Having the bronchoscopy was scary but very quick and simple. She had already had the minor Medi-port surgery before so it wasn't too unfamiliar, but we were still very nervous and hoped everything would go well. I was praying like never before. I didn't care how simple it was going to be. I still was worried about my baby who couldn't speak for herself and didn't comprehend anything happening to her. They brought us into a little room where they would administer the anesthesia and explain the procedure. While explaining the procedure she started to get a little anxious and started crying. They begin to give her a small amount of the anesthesia to calm her down. I was crying as usual. I was very emotional when it came to Jorgia; she was my heart. I was rubbing her little head telling her, "Its okay, mommy is right here.", as I always did. She started to relax.

Seeing how relaxed the anesthesia made her almost like she was drunk and very woozy, I knew it was best for her, but I didn't like seeing her that way. She looked like she was still trying to say mom, she was still trying to communicate with me, but the anesthesia wouldn't allow her to even say anything. I could tell she didn't like it at all.

She was looking at me like she wanted me to help her but there was nothing I could do. They started to wheel her away to the operating room as we stood in the hallway waving and saying goodbye Jorgia, we love you. When she was out of sight I broke down. I just wanted my baby to be well, I wanted to go home with my baby girl.

We stayed in the waiting room until surgery was over and waiting was brutal. It didn't take very long but for us it took forever. Everything involving Jorgia seemed to take longer than reality because we were always so tense and worried. Once the surgery was over, we were relieved to hear everything went perfectly and she had returned to her hospital room where she recovered very well. They still had to continue with breathing treatments and if we vowed to continue doing them at home this would allow us to go home in a couple of days. Trust me being in the hospital was starting to be part of our lives every year. In and out all the time was pretty much our new normal.

Chapter 11

Once we were able to go home from the hospital it was the best feeling ever, but we knew it was going to be a challenge at bedtime. The nights were tough with her. Jorgia would have a very difficult time sleeping and staying asleep at night. I just didn't know what to do. There were nights she wouldn't fall asleep until after 2 am. There were also times when she did go to sleep at a decent time, but she was still getting up and down all through the night. It was literally like having a newborn baby for years. I never got sleep, she never slept, my husband never slept. We were so drained the next day it was like trying to function on fumes. Some days we might have slept only two hours all night. Sometimes people would say, "Well why don't you sleep while she's at school"? That still was impossible. I had to come home and clean, pay bills, run errands, and get dinner prepared for the night. I still had to be a wife and a mother. That never stopped because it was something I could never turn off.

Jorgia was pulling me in so many different directions. Sometimes I would pull the car over and just cry from being so exhausted. Half the time I didn't know if I was coming or going. I felt like I was always in a fog, like the world through my eyes had no color. There was always something going on or something to do. If it wasn't Jorgia it would be one of my other kids. There was no downtime in my world. I was running on an empty tank constantly. There was one particular evening I put Jorgia to bed, and we tried to go to bed. She was just not sleepy, and she wouldn't stay in bed. That night we literally watched the sun come up. I lost it. I was crying uncontrollably. I was screaming about how tired I was and how I just wanted to go to sleep; I just needed to close my eyes for a moment. My wonderful, amazing husband took me by the hand, laid me on the couch and told me to just close my eyes. He took it from there. I felt so bad knowing he had to go to work as well, but I didn't know what else to do. He felt so bad for me. He knew I was so drained and at my breaking point, all I could do was just cry and cry. I couldn't stop. I cannot believe we literally never got to sleep that night. This happened pretty often. I knew I had to speak with the doctor about some medication or something to help Jorgia rest. We were not going to survive if we didn't get some regular sleep. There was no way we would be able to function every day in this manner, something had to be done. Since we were so tired all the time from no sleep, when we did fall asleep sometimes it was hard to wake up.

Jorgia was probably no more than about four or five years old. One night she had slept for a couple of hours before morning came. I went into her room to get her up for school and noticed she was not in her bed. I freaked out and my heart dropped as the room was spinning. I knew the door was behind me and I needed to get out of it to go find her, but I couldn't move because I was thinking the worst. I finally turned around and started to go down the stairs to see where she was. I got down about four steps when I looked and realized the front door was wide open. I screamed to my husband, "The front door is open! Where is Jorgia?" I don't even know how I got down the rest of the stairs so quickly. I think I must have jumped the next 12 steps rather than walk down. When I got to the front door that was wide open just below the steps. I could see clearly through the screen an image standing in the middle of the street. I thought maybe I was dreaming; I wasn't comprehending what I was seeing to be reality. I quickly realized the image was Jorgia. I didn't want to bust out the door, scare her, and cause her to run. I knew I had to act fast. I swung the door open calling her name and she started smiling. I walked towards her very quickly and took her hand, walked her upon the curb, picked her up and held her so tight sobbing saying I'm sorry baby girl, I'm so sorry. I felt awful that I didn't hear her get up. I didn't want to even think about what could happen and what I would have done if something would have happened. Realizing what a tragedy that could have been, I had to go inside and try to calm down because that really had me shaking uncontrollably.

Once again I started to realize God still must love me to spare my princess' life. I know angels were watching over her and I'm so grateful that she was not hurt. We then as a family had to take precautions and safe proof our home for Jorgia which meant putting up an iron gate in the front, installing doorbell cameras, installing alarm systems, basically whatever we had to do to keep her safe because this just could not happen again. Having that feeling of being that close to almost losing my baby was unfortunately not an unfamiliar feeling. I am definitely a believer in angels because I also almost lost my baby boy when he was born.

Unfortunately, I went into labor unexpectedly when I was seven months pregnant with my son Garrison. I remember being home in the family room on the computer and my husband decided to go to bed early. I wasn't tired, so I decided to stay up while my other son Garyn played video games. As I was on the computer I started to experience some minor contractions. I thought nothing of it knowing I was only seven months into the pregnancy. As the night went on, the contractions seemed to get worse and longer. I told my son it was time for bed as I decided to try and lay down hoping it would stop. I laid down next to my husband and within minutes the contractions were coming stronger and stronger. I woke my husband up telling him something was wrong, he was shocked. "No way," he said. "It's too early." I told him I didn't know why but I thought I was in labor and needed to get to the hospital. He rushed me to Fresno Community Hospital.

When I arrived, they started to check me over, moving me around. There was so much commotion. I was so scared and confused as to what was happening. I laid there with the monitor on my belly as beeping sounds filled the room. My husband decided to go home thinking it was going to be a long night. I told him I would call him with any updates. Within minutes of him leaving, the doctor came in informing me that an emergency C section was going to have to be done immediately due to the baby heartbeat stopping. He was in distress, and they are going to have to get him out NOW!

I was beyond frightened. I started to shiver, and I wasn't even cold. Tears began to hit my pillow as my heart began to ache with fear because of the unknown and the fact that I had just lost a baby from a miscarriage less than a year ago. The pain was still fresh and now this. God, I just couldn't seem to catch a break. I called my husband who had literally just walked through the door of our home, I was in a full-blown panic and crying telling him to get back to the hospital NOW! They were about to perform the C section because the baby wasn't breathing. My husband just kept asking repeatedly, "RIGHT NOW?" Several times and I kept saying YES! When he arrived back at the hospital I was already in the room about to receive the epidural. He stood in the hallway listening to my gut wrenching screams. I just wanted my baby boy to be healthy and alive. I kept asking if he was going to die. Of course, their answer was, "We are doing the best we can," I lay on the table as my husband sat right next to me gripping my hand ever so tightly whispering in my ear, "Everything is going to be okay honey." I could hear him, but I wasn't sure if I believed him. I could feel a lot of pressure and pulling as they were extracting my baby boy from my belly.

They finally got him out and as they lifted him in the air above the barrier where I could see him, I noticed his tiny, three pound body was limp, his arms were dangling, and his little mouth was open. There was no life. Panic filled the room as doctors and nurses scrambled around the room. They had his lifeless body lying on a table across the room. We could only see the top of his head. I said to my husband, "Go see about him, go see if he's okay." He said to me, "I just can't." He couldn't bear the thought of seeing his son knowing we could possibly lose him. I understood as I still laid there watching them work on my son frantically. I still hadn't even heard him cry or make any sound for that matter. I was still lying there as they are sewing the fresh wound where my son was just ripped from my body.

As I laid there I witnessed a doctor with a long white coat come into the room chewing on something as if he was coming off of lunch. He walked over to the table where they were working on my son and asked, "What was going on?" You could hear the stress in their voices as they quickly replied, "We can't get him to breathe." The doctor quickly noticed some adjustments needed to be made. He immediately grabbed some things from them and started to make the proper adjustments. Within seconds after the adjustments were made, I heard the sound of my baby boy crying out. It was the best sound I have heard in my entire life. I was now crying tears of joy. The doctor turned and walked right back out of the room after my son began to cry. I never heard from him again. No one even knows who this doctor was, but I know it was definitely an angel that walked into that room and saved my son's life.

Of course, we now had a long road ahead of us because he was a preemie. He was in the hospital for about a month which was not very long. He recovered and did well so quickly the doctors and nurses were shocked and amazed at how fast his little body was recovering. My son Garrison came home the day before Thanksgiving. Before he came home I was going to see him every day. I began making trips to the hospital once I recovered, checking on him every day. I spent many days leaving the hospital crying not wanting to leave him. It was definitely a lot, but we made it through. I named him Garrison after Garrison Hurst who was an NFL Football player. I wanted to give him a strong name because he had to already be a strong young man to come through this. This whole experience definitely made me a strong believer in angels. All of this happened before Jorgia was born. Naturally after experiencing such a loss and going through such a traumatic event having my son I couldn't help being so overprotective of Jorgia.

Chapter 12

For the most part I had to learn Jorgia in and out. I had to understand every gesture and sound. What it meant, what she wanted. The more I understood her helped to make my life a lot easier. When I didn't understand or know what she wanted, life became a nightmare. As she got older the tantrums turned into rages. The thing I hate the most is when people always think they have the answer to what you should do or what you need to do. I know it may sound cliche, but you don't know what my life is like or what I'm going through until you've walked a mile in my shoes. Jorgia's tantrums would go from 0 to 100 really quick.

I remember one morning it was probably about 4 or 5 am. I awoke to Jorgia screaming and jumped out of my sleep which was nothing new. I ran into her room. She was throwing her body round and screaming, trying to bite herself, at times she would even scratch her scalp until it started to bleed. I took her downstairs which was a hard task as she tried grabbing things on the way down still screaming and now crying. I was still half asleep, not sure if I was dreaming. Not fully awake, I sat on the couch with Jorgia trying to calm her down as we watched TV. Nothing was working as she started biting the couch, throwing whatever she could get her hands on. I had to stay close to her because I didn't want her to hurt herself.

She would sometimes bang her head. She has chipped her tooth because of banging her mouth on the counter or sliding door. I sat there with my head in my hands wishing and praying that I could just get one more hour of sleep, wishing she would just stop. There was nothing I could do, I had to just let her go through whatever was causing her to be upset. That was so hard to do. As her mom I'm supposed to be able to console her or make everything better but with Jorgia I had lost total control of that. I envied people that took naps, or people that were able to just sleep in. Those were things I missed doing, never realizing how much those little things meant until I no longer was able to do them.

Mornings like this always meant it was just the start of a long day. These tantrums would last sometimes 30 minutes to an hour. They would happen a few times a day out of nowhere. When I say they were exhausting it's probably an understatement. I questioned God a lot. People would tell me all the time how strong I was and that God had chosen me for her. I didn't understand why I was chosen. I didn't want to be chosen and I was far from strong. At least that's what I thought. I was so angry at God; I was angry at the world. I felt I deserved better than this. I was a good person. I would see and hear about young girls having healthy babies, drug addicts having healthy babies. People that I felt were so undeserving were having perfectly healthy babies. Women were having beautiful baby girls giving them up for adoption, abandoning them, even killing them. All this fueled my anger.

Why would God give them such a beautiful gift and they didn't appreciate it? I found myself hating Jorgia for being here knowing she didn't ask to be here. I hated myself because of hating her and I couldn't figure out what I did wrong for God to have given me a child with such a horrific disease and a devastating mental disorder. I thought if I prayed and really apologized to God for anything I had done he would somehow work a miracle and make my baby girl all better. I knew it was possible. I heard about miracles being raised in church, and believed it was definitely possible.

I prayed every day but unfortunately the miracle never came. I would be in public or picking my kids up from school and would see all these beautiful little girls. I couldn't help but wonder what it would be like to have such a blessing and opportunity. I hated mothers that had those opportunities and experiences of putting their little girls in dance, cheer, pageants, all the girly things I knew I could never do. Getting our nails done having mother daughter outings would not be my reality. In the back of my mind I was hurting so deep and what hurts the most is it was out of my control. I would stand there sometime with tears in my eyes wanting what they had. I could be anywhere, and little girls would always catch my eye because I longed for that so badly. I couldn't talk to Jorgia or even ask her how her day went, what she wanted for dinner, what movie she wanted to watch, what was her favorite color, what did she dream about, or even what she wanted to be when she grew up. I had a million more questions I wanted to ask my daughter but sadly those questions would never get answered. I don't think a day went by that I didn't cry or have to go scream somewhere.

When I would look into her eyes I knew she was in there. I just wish I had the power to bring her out because I needed her more than she needed me. I had to find a way to keep moving because life for me I knew would never be the same. I was constantly depressed. I felt like my home became a prison. I couldn't work which was very important to me. Meeting new people and learning new things. I had dreams, I had goals I wanted to accomplish in life. But now it was all fading away very quickly. I lost my motivation and drive to even want to do anything.

Everything was always about my kids, especially Jorgia. She took up 90 percent of my time but I somehow managed to still be the mom and wife I needed to be. It was very difficult at times trying to compose myself to help kids with homework or even to just cook dinner. My husband worked all day everyday so when I would finally get a chance to talk to him after his long day, he would listen and be very understanding and consoling. He knew what was going on but only to a certain extent, he had to be the provider, so I didn't blame him. A lot of my life became a blur because I was just going through the motions. I was never living life. I was surviving Jorgia; I was surviving autism the best way I could. I sometimes even started to become jealous of my husband's job, jealous of the things he was able to do. Even starting to be a little envious that he wasn't the one dealing with Jorgia the way I was. I wanted him to truly understand but no one really did. I always felt my husband's job ruined everything.

My husband and I had plans to do things together we had never done before like riding in a plane or going to the snow, traveling to another state just things we wanted to accomplish together. He was put into a new position which required him to travel. He got to travel to Florida which meant he got to ride in an airplane. He had to attend meetings and luncheons, meeting new people, all the things I desired to do. I remember the night before he was leaving I would cry myself to sleep not only because he was about to have the experience I only dreamed about, but he was leaving me for four days. We had never really been apart like that, not even for a day. I woke up the next morning to drop him off at the airport and I could feel the tears coming into my eyes because the road got blurry. I tried to hold it together because I didn't want him to know how I really felt. He thought I was just sad he was leaving, and I was but not entirely. After dropping him off I cried all the way back home because I felt cheated.

I wanted to have this experience with my husband but now it was gone. His job also required other things like going out to lunch, playing golf, attending football games, things to make customers happy to win them over. I understood, but at the same time I hated the situation, and I hated his job for robbing me of those experiences. While in Florida he was even able to visit Disney World and he also got to attend the NFL Pro Bowl. What I felt was beyond hurt, my heart was shattered. I loved my husband, and I was very proud of him and his accomplishments that were well deserving but just couldn't help but feel angry that I was being left out. I really wanted us to enjoy those things together, especially it being our first time seeing those things and seeing new places. I wanted to see the look on his face and be with him for all of the first-time experiences, which was what I looked forward to. I eventually told him how I felt, and he definitely understood but there was nothing we could do. It was part of his job and I had to cope with those feelings and hope one day I will be able to make my dreams come true. My husband has done everything in his power to make me feel special, he was an amazing husband and he felt bad, I felt that way. I didn't want him to feel bad, but it was something I couldn't help. The things Jorgia did make my life unbearable to deal with sometimes.

I can remember Jorgia was in diapers until she was about eleven years old. It was like having a baby for eleven years. I used to try potty training her and it all became a total nightmare. Jorgia moved very quickly, the damage she could do in a manner of minutes was incredible. I would put her on the toilet and clean her up, then walk away for a minute or two to grab clean clothing, only to come back to a horrifying scene. In the bathroom when I got to the door she had ripped up her pee and poop diaper all over the bathroom. When she got older these diapers would now have blood in them. Disgusting I know, trust me I wanted to throw up, but I had to put aside my feelings and do what I needed to do. I cried, trying hard not to fight the nauseating feeling in the pit of my stomach. If you understand when ripping a diaper, the little gel beds stick to everything, and they were sticking to me as I wiped. It seemed like the more I tried to wipe up the more they multiplied. She had shit literally everywhere. On the floor, rugs, her hands, her hair, and other places I didn't know it could go. She was rubbing her hands together like it was lotion. I didn't even know where to begin. I didn't know if I should run, cry, or throw up. I chose to just keep crying, spraying, and wiping. That's all I could do.

I took a deep breath after a 30-minute clean-up process only for her to do it again several times a day. I felt my body aging at a very fast pace. There were days I felt I never stopped moving. I found myself looking forward to her going to school or to the autism center just to get a break. Even then it was hard to relax because now I had to clean up, prepare dinner, pay bills, or go to a doctor's appointment. There was never a break, my calendar was so full I could no longer recognize what day it was or the holidays. Caring for

Jorgia was becoming way more than I expected. I found myself sometimes searching and calling to get information on possible facilities to place her because I didn't think I could do this much longer. I was definitely having mixed feelings because this was still my baby girl and I didn't want to just drop her off or leave her somewhere. I guess I was looking for some sort of relief. I was scared, I was tired, I was angry all the time. I had lost myself; I hadn't felt like myself in such a long time. I needed to find me but didn't know how or where to begin. I was starting to realize I may be caring for Jorgia for the rest of her life, and I just wanted options because I was not getting younger. When you see Jorgia you would never think she was capable of the things I was experiencing.

Chapter 13

Jorgia didn't look like she had autism, she looked like a normal little girl, so it would break my heart when people tried to talk to her or ask her questions and she would just stare at them. I had to explain to them that she was autistic. When Jorgia was about twelve she was pretty much potty-trained except for wearing diapers at night and having occasional accidents. In the back of my mind, I started to worry about puberty. I was seeing her body beginning to develop. I got a lump in my throat because I knew we were about to enter a whole new unknown chapter of Jorgia's journey. Jorgia was not your typical teenager, but her body still couldn't resist her development not just physically but mentally as well. The tantrums were already out of control; the car rides were just becoming a very intense drive. I was always afraid of the unexpected with her.

I remember pulling over on the side of the road as tears covered my face as if I just emerged from a pool of water. I was just trying to come to grips that I was just attacked by my daughter, and it truly felt like I had been in the boxing ring with Mike Tyson. Jorgia's blows were far from a child's. They were strong, hard hits that hurt like hell. She would be screaming so loud my ears wouldn't stop ringing for days. Jorgia was swinging at me, biting the seal belt, and she would bite chunks out of the interior of the car. When she was younger she would bite chunks out my dashboard and steering wheel while we would be sitting in the car waiting for something.

I would seat belt her in, but she would find a way out. I would look at people in other cars wondering if they could see or hear what was going on, and they seemed to have no idea. If they only knew what I was going through in this car they wouldn't believe it. When I would finally drop her off at school or the center, I would have to pull over, take a minute and cry that ugly cry as they would call it. I would scream and pray sometimes my only word to God would be WHY?! I really wanted this question answered but I was starting to think God was angrier with me than I thought and probably didn't appreciate me for always asking WHY? I know he had a job for me, I know God was trying to carve a path for me I needed to take, I know I was taught to never question God because he knew what he was doing but This situation was making me doubt everything I was taught.

One time I thought I was going to die. Jorgia had just been released from a hospital stay. My husband and son had left ahead of us with all of our belongings from a 16-day stay known as the "Tune Up." Jorgia and I got into the car and headed home. Halfway home she started to tantrum. I was in disbelief that this was happening right now. Somehow she managed to get her seat belt off. She came from behind me while I was driving, and she grabbed a handful of my hair and yanked it as hard as she could and held on. You know autistic kids are stronger than a typical person their age. I couldn't move my head at all. I think my heart stopped beating. I was paralyzed with fear because I could no longer see the road, so I hit the brakes. That was a big mistake. I soon realized I was on the freeway and cars were probably behind me going to plow right into the back of me. I quickly hit the gas again with Jorgia still holding on to my hair. I managed to pull over off to the side of the freeway. I then started to try and peel her fingers open hoping to loosen her grip to let my hair go. Finally, I was able to pry my hair loose from her hands, as cars were zooming by at probably 60 to 70 mph. Trying to time the cars correctly I had to jump out of the car, so I could put her back in the seat belt hoping that would slow down the attack. My body was already exhausted from the long hospital stay, and now I couldn't even make it home before the nightmare began. I was able to get out of the car and opened the back door where Jorgia was sitting and still screaming. As soon as I opened the door and bent down to grab the seat belt she snatched my glasses off my face and threw them behind me onto the freeway. Thank goodness no cars were coming at that time, so I was able to grab them very quickly and get back to the car where I proceeded to buckle her back in and try to get home safely.

These types of encounters with Jorgia in the car were becoming more and more frequent. I was completely terrified to get in the car with my own daughter, I would try to avoid any car rides unless necessary. No one knows what it feels like to be afraid of your own child who at the same time doesn't have a clue what they are doing. You can't even begin to figure them out. It hurts so bad when she tries to attack me when I'm trying to help her or console her. That just breaks my heart. Jorgia moves very quickly, and her aggression is very powerful. The strength she has is unbelievable. She would fight and try to hurt you as if she had no idea who you were. For me as her mom it was very painful. All I wanted to do is help her but every time I would get close to her during a time when she wasn't feeling well, in pain, or just frustrated she would fully attack me.

I would've never guessed she could do the things she was doing. She would try biting me as I held her hand, she would try head butting me when I would get too close, she would scratch and pinch me. I know she was only searching for relief, but it was very disturbing to see your child in this state. I was so tired of crying but that was all I could do. My body would feel so beat up, my arms and hands would be scratched up, sometimes bleeding. My feet and hands would be throbbing because I also was dealing with arthritis. My knees would ache so bad from standing for long periods and going rounds with her, and my back was so stiff I could hardly stand up straight. The feeling of looking into her eyes as she was having a tantrum or attacking was overwhelming. Her eyes were just dark, like she was somewhere else. It was almost like the Incredible Hulk scenario, where she would seem to become someone else.

The crazy part about the whole thing is she would come out of it like nothing ever happened. Jorgia would be laughing and playing, literally back to herself while I was still standing there in disbelief trying to catch my breath wondering what just happened. I had to snap out of it as well until the next episode, not knowing when that would be. I was confused and frustrated. I knew that at her age she was dealing with hormones. Jorgia was starting to become a young lady. I began seeing her breasts development and pubic hair. I immediately knew that starting her period was right around the corner. I remembered when I was becoming a young lady, developing breasts it was very painful and uncomfortable for me. My breast would be sore so I could imagine Jorgia was probably experiencing the same thing. The only difference is she wasn't able to communicate how she was feeling at all. I think these kinds of issues were beginning to feed her aggression. She wasn't understanding her body changes and with that came attitude changes as well. We bumped heads constantly.

Just because Jorgia had autism didn't mean she couldn't have an attitude. Just like a typical teenager, she wanted what she wanted when she wanted it.

The way she communicated was through aggression, that's why her going to the center and learning how to communicate things the right way was good for her and very important. She didn't like being pushed out of her comfort zone or made to do things unfamiliar. When I would see her go through these stages It really felt like a knife through my heart. Jorgia wasn't this bad when she was younger. She really had changed drastically over time.

I didn't notice right away but Jorgia had regressed a lot over the years. When she was younger she would dance, she would walk around the house in my shoes which were five times her size, she would try to sing, she would jump around. She seemed more alive, she seemed more aware and happier. Now that Jorgia was older you would never know she even knew how to do any of those things at all. As a family we took many pictures and videos of family outings, gatherings, having fun at home, even just to record when the kids were doing something funny or crazy. Going back reminiscing on some of the photos and videos my husband happened to run across a video of Jorgia dancing and trying to sing into a microphone we bought her for Christmas.

He sent me the video and I was stunned. Why doesn't she do any of those things now? Her dad even took her to the father daughter dance, and she had an amazing time on the dance floor twirling and singing to "Let it go" which was a popular song at that time from the movie "Frozen." I couldn't believe what I was seeing and now I was concerned about why she regressed so much. It was definitely disappointing and made me want answers. Why with all the therapy and early intervention this has happened? Is it normal? Will she regain what she has lost? There was so much I needed to find out, it was somewhat devastating to see her decline.

Chapter 14

My husband and I constantly discussed as we were getting older what we would do with Jorgia. It was a very difficult subject but certainly needed. I loved my daughter more than life itself. The last thing I ever wanted to do was give my baby up or let someone else take care of her. I was very overprotective of her, and it would be out of the question for me to let her go, but I was running out of answers. I just don't know If I could continue to care for her needs. Especially with her getting bigger and stronger I wasn't sure If I could keep up with her. I was becoming a little afraid, I was completely torn. I didn't want to place her with anyone, anywhere but in reality that may be an option we would have to consider given the circumstances. I just didn't want to face that fact. I was feeling very frustrated as well because you hear all the time about early intervention for autism is the best thing, catching it early can prevent a lot of other issues. Well, I won't say it isn't true, but I will say for my daughter it really didn't seem to make a difference. I was very hopeful the interventions would eventually pay off, but for now, they never seemed to help. I was disappointed to see absolutely no change. If anything, she got worse or regressed. There were some good things that came from it that probably could have happened through regular therapy, like hearing her speak for the first time, seeing her learn new things. They seemed like small victories, but it wasn't enough for me to say early intervention mattered.

I found myself always on the internet after being told by her doctor not to do that. It was extremely hard not to search for information. Who else could

I turn to for answers? For guidance? For support? Besides my husband who knew very little and no time to learn much because of his job. I had the time to read a lot and watch numerous videos. Sometimes I just wanted to see if anyone out there was going through the same things I was experiencing. What did they do? How did they overcome certain issues? I wanted to see how they were coping, how they felt, if anyone mentioned any resources that would help in any way. I became so obsessed; I would scare myself after seeing horrifying videos of parents trying to manage tantrums. It was all I had to go on.

I came across this one video that sticks in my head, every time I think about it my stomach hurts and I feel my eyes tearing up. I cried so much more than I ever had in my lifetime. I was extremely emotional when it came to my daughter and her autism. On this video I saw a mother with a teenage son who was very big for his age, which meant he also had to be very strong. He had severe autism, and it began to show him having a tantrum and the mom started screaming for her husband to come help. As she was waiting for her husband this poor kid was slinging his mom all over the room. She was trying with every fiber in her body to at least get him on the ground. He just wouldn't go down. This mom continued to scream with so much fear in her voice. Her and her son were screaming, and he was hitting himself in the head with his own closed fist. It was so hard to watch. With tears beginning to drip from my face and onto the keys of my laptop I continued to watch the video that had my heart racing. The father finally entered the room after about two minutes which must have seemed like a lifetime to the mom. He tried to assist the mother in getting their son to the ground. After about 30 minutes of fighting and struggling with their son they managed to finally take him down. He fell to the ground landing flat on his belly. It was like watching someone take down a wild beast. I was very familiar with the situation. While this kid was on the ground the father persisted to put his knee into the middle part of back so he couldn't move or try to get up. They held him there for about 20 minutes until he was able to calm down and the mother was able to catch her breath.

This was just one of many videos I watched, and I was so alarmed at what the future held for me and my daughter. I wasn't trying to scare myself, but I guess deep down inside I wanted to learn as much as possible. I was trying to educate myself with whatever information I could find. I was also trying to prepare myself for things I didn't know could happen. My husband always said if you stay ready you will never have to get ready. It was something he learned through football, but it really does apply to whatever you want. I was trying to always stay ready.

I was consumed in researching Autism information as well as Cystic Fibrosis. It was so overwhelming my head was spinning and migraines had become more consistent. I became a nervous wreck. I started to realize I was bracing myself for the things I was seeing on these videos, but they never happen when you expect, nothing Jorgia did was ever expected. It's always unexpected and I was never ready. Taking care of Jorgia really took me out of the norm, and out of my comfort zone. Most of all it was hard as a mom to admit I no longer had the control I thought I had over the situation. Nothing about my life was no longer normal, especially sleep. I was so sleep deprived on most days; I didn't even hardly remember what I had done that day. I could hardly stay awake during those days. I found myself falling asleep sitting at traffic lights. I heard my son saying "Mom, go!" It was scary because I didn't want to end up harming my other kid due to my exhaustion. I would immediately wake up in a panic hoping I didn't hurt my children or anyone else. I had to do something. This situation could not continue.

Jorgia had a primary doctor from birth until about 6 years old, who saw her on a regular basis. He had her on a few medications that seemed to work for a little while. Her sleep was always a problem. I was hoping the doctor could prescribe something to help her sleep, but nothing was working. She would sleep for a few hours here and there but never all night. She would wake up constantly and since I was exhausted I would just put her in bed with me just to get as much sleep as possible. Later in the night I would sneak and put her back in her room in her own bed. Within an hour or two she was back. This went on night after night after night. I was probably getting a total of maybe four hours of sleep. It was almost impossible to function on a daily basis, especially taking care of an autism child but I had no choice. I was doing the best I could with what I knew. Eventually a few years down the road her doctor suggested I find another doctor that specializes more in children like her as well as a medical management doctor who could manage her medications. Perhaps he could prescribe something that may work better for her. I agreed and my research began again.

I made several phone calls, asking around for recommendations. I heard about a doctor that was very good at the same hospital where Jorgia was being treated for her Cystic Fibrosis at "Valley Children's Hospital at the Charlie Mitchell Clinic." I called immediately and scheduled an appointment. When I finally got in to see Dr. Hailey Nelson, she was everything I hoped for and more. She was patient, caring, always smiling, and even gave Jorgia a brand new beautiful plush blanket and a toy. She wanted to do anything she could to help my daughter and that was music to my ears. I was excited and looking forward to working with her. I was also still searching for a medical management doctor who was a child psychologist. Once again I heard about a doctor that was very good who could probably see her right away and put her on the right meds. I called immediately and made an appointment to see him as soon as possible.

This appointment was very important in regard to her sleeping pattern and behavior. I hoped he could help prescribe something to help her calm down and eventually sleep better so I could start to be a better me. I wanted to be the best version of myself for her and the only way to do that is to get more rest. I finally got in to meet the Child Psychologist, Dr. Alimysuia. He was very thorough in explaining to me the treatment he wanted to try for Jorgia. He turned his computer screen around to show me his plan.

The first thing he wanted to do (which I thought was very interesting) was to do a DNA test to see if the meds she was taking were right for her. These would also show the meds she should be on. I felt a little darkness starting to lift. I could see a little light beginning to break through. I was very hopeful during that appointment. Jorgia was there with me crying and starting to tantrum because she wanted to leave. Appointments were always extremely difficult because I would miss some important information the doctor said because I was trying to calm her down or keep her entertained in some way. I tried to listen and take in as much as I could. Jorgia just didn't like being anywhere but home, school, and her center anywhere else we would have problems.

The DNA test was ordered and now we had to wait for the results. A few weeks went by, and I received a phone call from Dr. Alymisua's office informing me that the test results were in. I needed to make an appointment to speak with him again. With no hesitation I scheduled the appointment, and the anticipation was killing me. When the day finally arrived, I couldn't get to the psychologist office quick enough. I sat in the waiting room praying to God who I thought hated me for some reason but was hoping he would have mercy on me today. I was hoping this would be the beginning of some relief for not just me but our family. I dealt with Jorgia 99% of the time, but this affected our entire family in many ways. I was pacing the floor of the waiting room, not able to be still. I was anxious, excited, nervous, most of all I was tired and ready for change. They finally called my name. I decided to take Jorgia to the Autism center that day so I would be able to give the doctor my full attention and grasp every word he said. When I sat down my heart was beating so hard and fast I could actually hear it in my ears as they began pulsating from my rapid heartbeat. He had the results spread across his desk as he began to tell me what everything meant.

There were three columns on this paper and each column represented a color red, green, and black. All the medications listed in the red column were the medications she should not be on or should stay away from. All the medications listed in the green column were the medications she should be or needed to be taking. All the medications listed in the black column were not bad or good; they were just medications that may or may not work. He turned the paper to me as he started to explain that all the medication Jorgia was currently taking was all listed in the RED column. I was stunned, my eyes got so big, and my mouth dropped open so wide my hand couldn't even cover my entire mouth. I just couldn't believe this whole time she was not on the right medication.

The only thing that was keeping me from getting too angry is that we were there to get answers. Now I was ready to get the ball rolling in the right direction. The doctor put Jorgia on a few anti-psychotic medications accompanied by a few over the counter medications to offset the anti-psychotic meds or balance everything out. There were so many meds, but I was scared but at this point and willing to try anything. After finding out she had been taking the wrong meds this long, it took a few months of trial and error to adjust the dosages higher or lower. We had to start with small milligrams and slowly move up or down, so it wasn't 100% effective at first.

The nights were still challenging. I was lying there sleeping one night, maybe about 2am in the morning actually. I was in a deep sleep which was becoming pretty frequent because I was always so exhausted. I felt a presence. I don't know why but something was telling me to open my eyes and when I did Jorgia was literally just standing there over me just staring at me. It scared the hell out of me. I jumped up so quickly and I was still out of it. I was stumbling and out of breath. Jorgia didn't do anything but the fact that she was standing there freaked me out. I now slept with one eye open. It became harder to sleep soundly because I was so afraid she might be standing over me again. It was always in the back of my mind.

Other nights when she would wake up like she was running from something, and the sound was like thunder. When this would occur sometimes it would be a few hours after putting her to bed. I would be downstairs preparing dinner or eating dinner. I would have to run back upstairs to put her back to bed. I could hear when she got up. It sounded like the ceiling was going to collapse. You could hear the walls cracking. She awoke with such force it made me react so quickly I couldn't move fast enough. This happened almost every night.

I clearly remember most nights I was sound asleep, and I could hear the thunder of her jumping out of bed. She swung her door open to her room as the doorknob hit the back of the wall, sounding as if the whole house shook. Honestly, it was like an earthquake shaking the house. She would then reach our bedroom door, which was cracked open, and push the door open so hard, it sounded as if it went through the wall. I sat up in bed so quickly out of my sleep thinking I must have been dreaming. Still not fully comprehending what was going on for a split second, I didn't know if we were being robbed or about to be attacked. It literally woke up the entire house. As soon as I realized it was just Jorgia getting out of bed I immediately hit the floor running trying to get her back to sleep which sometimes took about an hour or two.

There were nights I didn't get back to bed until four or five in the morning. This went on for what seemed like forever. The times she did get up through the night made it like a nightmare getting up and down out of my sleep. I would wake up in such a panic because for a split second I didn't realize where I was or what was going on. It was like my mind had to catch up with my body and what my eyes were seeing. This would trigger unbearable migraines that made me sick to my stomach, my eyes would feel as if they had sand in them all day from a lack of sleep.

Jorgia would even crawl over me to lay between me and my husband which was always an uncomfortable situation. The bigger she got the worse it was. I was completely hanging off the side of the bed just trying to at least close my eyes to get any sleep I could possibly get. My husband was also feeling the exhaustion from being awakened every time this occurred. He would be running on fumes at work the next day. This is really taking a toll on all of us. I was hoping autism wouldn't become our demise.

This one particular morning right before it was time to get up, the house was very quiet as we laid there sleeping sound. I kept hearing an occasional boom sound. I turned to my husband just as his eyes were opening, asking him, "Did you hear that boom sound?" He said yes but wasn't sure what it was. We laid there to see if it would stop, and it went on and on. My husband got up and proceeded down the hallway to see if he could hear where it was coming from. When he got in the hallway my son Garrison was coming out of his room where he met my husband in the hallway standing there trying to figure out what this mysterious sound was. I was sitting up in the bed where I could clearly see into the hallway. We could all still hear the boom sounds. My husband looked back at me and said he thought it was coming from Jorgia's room where he then noticed her light was on. I told him to peek in there to see if she was OK. I saw him open the door with my son standing behind him as if they were entering a lion's den. My husband opened her door slowly and all I could see was him and my son's mouth drop open like they had just seen a ghost.

I couldn't get up fast enough as I was wrapped up in the covers. It was pissing me off because the covers prevented me from moving as quickly as I wanted. I finally managed to get to my feet not knowing what to expect. I started toward Jorgia's door asking, "What is it? What happened?" but they wouldn't answer me. The two of them just stood there shaking their heads. When I got to the door and looked in I felt my knees buckle and my blood pressure must have gone through the roof because my head was throbbing. I was pissed off and in a straight state of shock at what Jorgia had done. She had thrown every trophy that was displayed beautifully on her shelf, onto the floor. They were all shattered and broken into pieces. Her crowns were thrown around and broken as well leaving the shelves completely bare. The wooden plaques from her pageants were on the floor as well. The DVD player was hanging from her shelf by a cord. Pictures were thrown around broken. I was angry, because the pageant trophies I worked so hard for her to win were shattered to pieces. This was the only thing we had done together that gave me that feeling of normalcy. I was hurt to see what she had done. I know she didn't understand the full extent of her actions, but my heart couldn't separate her understanding from what I was feeling. I wanted to cry but there was no time to cry. Among all this mess sat Jorgia in the middle of her bed smiling like nothing had happened. My husband and son helped me clean up the mess as we were just all in disbelief at what she was capable of doing.

We still had to manage getting my boys up early and ready for school. It was frustrating and draining to say the least. Eventually I had to work with the therapist to try and break her from my bed because there was no way we could keep this up. We were getting to a point where it was becoming even harder to function. Something had to change and slowly over time it got worse before it got better trying to break her from this habit. She wanted to get in my bed, but I had to keep telling her no as I would have to keep taking her back to her room and making sure she would stay. There were many nights of absolutely no sleep before we started to see improvement. I was able to return to the psychologist's office to discuss increasing the dosage on her medication because she still wasn't sleeping. The tantrums would still happen on a regular basis but not as aggressively.

When we finally reached a dose that worked to keep Jorgia asleep. I was happy but a little taken back at how much medication she was on. I was concerned but I had to do something. There was no way I could continue to live this way. Jorgia's medication in the morning consisted of 26mg Invega pills which were anti-psychotic meds, 1-20 mg of Geodon that was also an anti-psychotic medication, 1 Methyl Folate which was used to help make other meds work to their maximum potential, 1 Loratadine for allergies, 1 Famotidine for acid reflux. After school about 3pm she would then take 2 -.01 mg Clonidine and .01 2 mg Clonidine ER. The regular Clonidine we were hoping would start to relax her as well as make her just a little tired before bed. The Clonidine ER was an extended release that would release into her bloodstream slowly through the day making her sleepy by the time bedtime came around. It also helped to calm her down just a little. At around 6pm we would finish up her daily meds with 3-80mg Geodon, 3-10mg of

Melatonin which is a natural drug our body already makes. Sometimes it doesn't make enough to help keep us asleep and Jorgia's body was just not making enough. She also took 10 or 11 .01 mg of clonidine which is a very low dose. That is the reason she took so many, as well as 2 more .01 mg Clonidine ER. This now was her daily medication routine.

It was very overwhelming but surprisingly Jorgia was great at taking pills which made everything much easier. She took them every day with no problem. Her sleep pattern began to get better with the exception of those times when she wasn't feeling well or bed wetting which was typical. I didn't mind that at all, as long as my sleep wasn't being disturbed on a nightly basis. Even though I began to get better rest the exhaustion never left. Every day I still felt as if I was still trying to catch up on sleep. I knew with as much as I had lost I would probably never catch up.

Jorgia days were long, from driving her to school every morning, picking her up after school, then packing another backpack for the Autism center where she would go for her behavioral therapy. I always had to pack changing clothes and her lunch and things like that. Even though she was older she would still have accidents. Jorgia was probably beginning to use the bathroom on her own about the age of 11 or 12. She wouldn't poop on herself which made me happy, but she would still pee on herself. It took a while to finally get her to say potty whenever she had to pee.

I was on pins and needles knowing she would soon start her period. I started making appointments with her doctor and a Gynecologist to discuss my options for her because I didn't know what I was going to do or what she was going to do or how she would react for that matter. I just knew I had to start preparing. I started to see discharge in her underwear. I was just flustered and anxious. I was in panic mode every day waiting for that dreadful period. I was literally shaking every time she had to go potty. I was cringing. Even though she was pretty much potty-trained Jorgia was not able to clean herself. That was always something I had to do for her, so with every wipe I held my breath.

I would tell my husband all the time how afraid I was of her starting her period. He would always try to talk to me and tell me not to worry. He constantly tried to make me understand that I was doing all the right things. He said I was strong and considering what I had already been through, this was nothing. He was always so supportive and positive not to mention he was always right. He was truly my sounding board as well as my best friend. I would always calm down after talking to him, only for the fear to come back as soon as the thought entered my mind. I was stressing out completely.

Speaking with the doctor she would always reassure me everything would be fine. I asked if she could take something to prevent her period from even coming because I was so stressed over this. The doctor said she couldn't do that because they would need her to have a period to make sure nothing else medically was going on. She told me they dealt with this in autistic children all the time. She gave me a few options to consider for Jorgia. One option was the pill every day and the other options were the patch or an implant. After several discussions and careful thinking, I decided when it was time I would do the pills. With the pills you had more control. If they do an implant and she has a reaction or something it would be a whole situation I didn't want to even deal with and I didn't think the patch would be as effective.

One morning I was rushing around getting Jorgia ready for school. She went to the potty and pulled her underwear down and I saw red!! I heard my heart hit the floor. I was screaming, "Oh No! Oh NO!" over and over. My husband yelled "what's wrong?" I yelled back with that crack in my voice as if I was about to cry. Jorgia started her period." he said. OH NO! Now my thoughts were racing. I didn't know if she was cramping, if she felt moody, if she felt sick. I immediately grabbed my phone to call the doctor only to realize it was still so early in the morning the office wasn't even open yet. I wanted to cry. I felt so alone and terrified. I took a deep breath and tried to gather myself and began to clean her up.

I then went and grabbed a bag of pads and put one on her. It didn't seem to bother her to wear it, I think because she wore pull ups at night it probably didn't feel any different. Now I really wished she could talk to me! This was a very important moment in her life. This was a very important and scary moment in my life as well and I couldn't even have a conversation with my daughter who was becoming a young lady. She wasn't even aware of what was happening to her. It's life moments like this that made me start to think about Jorgia's quality of life. These thoughts would make me feel so sad and depressed. Now reality was setting in that my daughter would never get married, never have children. These thoughts were making my head hurt but they wouldn't stop coming. She will never know what it's like to have true love, she won't get to experience her prom, go to college, be able to work, live on her own, the list just goes on and on and on….

I finally got a hold of the doctor that informed me to bring her in after her period to start her on the birth control pills immediately. The pills would stop her periods. Jorgia's period wasn't very heavy and lasted a few days. I was so grateful for that part. I just made sure I gave her pain medication just in case she was experiencing any discomfort or pain I wasn't aware of. Jorgia had a high tolerance for pain though, so it was very hard to read her. Once her period stopped It felt like a big weight being lifted off my shoulders, I felt like I could walk lighter, the worry of it all was really weighing me down.

I got her to the doctor who prescribed her Daysee which is a birth control tablet she added to her morning medication. This made it easy for me not to forget to give to her. There were a few times I did forget to give to her, and she would start to spot during her scheduled period time. Other than that, this was just one more thing we were able to overcome with many more to go.

Chapter 15

The small accomplishments are what motivated me to keep going. You really don't realize how strong you are or what you can get through until you're actually going through it or once you come out on the other side. If I would have been told I would be raising a daughter with Autism and Cystic fibrosis and the challenges I would face I wouldn't have believed it. If I had a choice I would have run as fast as I could because I would have thought I wouldn't be strong enough to get through. But so far, taking one day at a time is becoming my new normal. I have become so passionate as a mom advocating for my daughter and many others I had touched.

Sometimes wanting to get out of the house was a task. Jorgia was not social at all. Even when around other kids or people she would rather watch and listen but not want to be a part of anything going on. One thing about Jorgia is she always maintains very good eye contact which isn't typical of autistic kids. I wasn't sure if she understood her surroundings. I always had to keep a close eye on her when around other children because she would definitely try to attack if they got too close or took something she was playing with. That would set her off and cause her to attack. Jorgia moved very quickly and was very strong when it came to her aggression. I could tell she would get a little jealous when other children were around me which was typical of any child. I was learning over the years caring for an autistic child and their issues was never a quick fix. Everything took time, planning, parent training and much more. I never thought I would have to be trained on how to care for my own child.

It was hard to let people into our lives, it was uncomfortable, it almost felt a little degrading and embarrassing at times. I didn't want to be told what to do and how to do it, but I needed help because I didn't know it all when it came to her. I was getting older, and my body was not as young as it used to be. I was feeling every ache and pain I never felt before. I hurt places I didn't know I could hurt. I felt worn down and Jorgia's life was just beginning. I have heard my whole life that "God won't put more on you than you can bear," I used to believe that but since having Jorgia I'm not sure how much more I can bear.

I have tried doing things with my husband like taking small vacations, spending a night or two away. Every time we would get away I was checking in on Jorgia constantly. I wasn't just worried about her; I was also worried about whoever was watching her because I knew what it took to watch her. It was very hard to take my mind off her because I spent so much time consumed in her world I no longer knew how to be present in mine. Sometimes the babysitter would call to ask me a question, and every single time my phone would ring my heart would drop.

One particular weekend for our anniversary, I remember my husband and I decided to go up to the casino to just get away from it all and relax and have a little fun. The ride was probably about 40 minutes. We were enjoying each other's conversation, laughing, and reminiscing on our life so far, which made the ride not seem so long. I was excited to get out of the house and take a little time for myself. We reached the casino and went in to start enjoying the evening. We grabbed some drinks and sat down at a slot machine and started playing. It was so nice to hear all the people around talking, laughing, and yelling. It was these sounds that I don't get to hear very often. All these things are what I was going to do tonight. I was going to relax and loosen up from such an intense year. Within a few minutes of our arrival before my seat even warmed up, my phone rang. It was my daughter, who was watching

Jorgia at the time.

My heart sank to my feet. I answered very quickly as a feeling had come over me like I knew something was wrong. I was right!! My daughter Shana was calling to inform me Jorgia was vomiting and wouldn't stop. I just couldn't believe it; I just couldn't catch a damn break. My daughter continued to apologize, the sadness in her voice was painful to hear. She tried not to call us because she didn't want to ruin our trip. I proceeded to tell her not to worry, it's OK and we were on our way.

I hung up the phone with complete and utter disappointment, we jumped to our feet, walking with urgency to get to the car. All the excitement I felt was gone, all the feeling in my body did a complete 160. I was now filled with worry, planning my next steps as we hurried down the mountain as quickly as possible. I was texting her with constant updates on our whereabouts and she was texting back with updates on Jorgia. I knew when I got home I was going to have to head to the hospital. I was in for another long night…..maybe longer! When I finally arrived home I quickly got her to the hospital where they were able to start the IV process to keep her hydrated. It was definitely another horrible experience, but nothing new to us. She eventually recovered and was back home within a week or so. These types of incidents occurred periodically; you just never knew when it was going to transpire. It was a chance we had to continue to take. It became impossible to find babysitters for Jorgia that I trusted. My daughter Shana was amazing. She never minds someone watching her, but I felt she had her own life, and I didn't want to always count on her or get in the way of anything she had planned.

When Jorgia was younger we had a babysitter that started watching her. We trusted her because she used to also be one of Jorgia therapists. When she left her job she stayed around and became close to our family. She was absolutely heaven sent. Having her around I was able to do more things especially attending my son Garyn football games, and football camps that were sometimes out of town. My husband and I were also able to take a title more time for date nights and things like that. When she wasn't available, finding back up was never successful. That's how I knew if we ever lost her it was going to be a problem. My husband and I decided in 2019 to plan a vowel renewal because we had never had a wedding before. I don't know how I was able to do it, but I was proud of myself for all my hard work I put into this vowel renewal. We wanted to have a wedding years ago but that didn't go well.

During the planning process we paid a caterer that ran off with our money, so we had to cancel the wedding, it was devastating. Nevertheless, we were excited for this opportunity to do it now, which was going to be bigger and better. I'm a true believer that things happen for a reason. I was making a lot of things myself to save money, it was fun but yet time consuming. I was running around getting invitations done, meeting with decorators, trying to get the wedding party together for fittings. It was complete chaos, but exciting chaos.

Going through all this of course in my mind I was so stressed about how Jorgia was going to act. She was definitely in the wedding. I wanted to make her a flower girl, but I was scared she would try to rip or eat the rose petals. I decided instead of a flower girl I would have her walk in right before me with a white rustic sign hanging around her neck that read "Daddy, here comes mommy." If she was able to pull this off I knew she would steal the hearts of everyone there. Although I was still worried sick, I wanted her to be a part of our special day no matter what. I was trying to have faith that she would do great. The babysitter was there helping out, I couldn't have done this without her. She got her dressed and everything. She stayed with her the whole time. She made our special day possible for us and I was grateful in every way.

The time came for Jorgia to come down the aisle, I wasn't there to see her of course, I was still getting ready for my grand entrance. I heard she did amazing. I was so proud of her that it felt like my heart was going to burst. I couldn't wait to see all the photos and videos of her one beautiful moment. Surprisingly, Jorgia did incredible the whole night. I was so pleased with what we accomplished. The babysitter had to leave because we didn't plan on her staying with Jorgia the whole night. I wish it was something we would have thought about, but it was too late. It was our wedding night and guess who slept right between us at the hotel. Well, it was almost a perfect night, but it was close enough, and I was satisfied. I'll take it every time, because knowing what Jorgia was capable of, it could have been a total disaster.

Unfortunately, later down the road we had to let our babysitter go. I didn't want to, but it was a decision we had to make in the best interest of our family. We went out one night and the babysitter was there along with my older children. She decided to invite a male friend over without our permission. My older children thought we knew because this babysitter was like family. She told us everything. She always asked before having company over, which is what made his situation very confusing. This particular time she didn't ask or inform us about anything. However, we saw this individual on our camera footage and questioned the babysitter and she didn't deny anything. I still didn't want to let her go because I knew how hard it would be to find someone like her. My husband was in a different state of mind as a man, and insisted we let her go. To have a male in his home, who he didn't know, without our permission, around our children was unforgivable. I had to agree so the decision was made. It's been a struggle ever since because in reality she is irreplaceable but what she did was unforgettable. I even started researching again trying to find places that will allow us to drop her off at least for the day or weekend but everywhere I called just didn't take adolescents, only adults.

This actually made me angry because there was just no place out there for us parents to turn to. I wish I could open a place like that for parents with disabled children or parents with autistic children. It was something our community needed and was lacking. Resources for parents like me were lacking, period. This may be something I will consider looking into in the near future. After losing my babysitter I started to feel trapped again, having those depressing feelings, feeling jealous of my husband because once again I couldn't do anything I wanted. It felt like Groundhog Day again every day. I didn't have friends because it was hard to make friends, especially when you didn't get out much. I was never in the right places to build those relationships with people.

Chapter 16

My husband and I started having hard conversations, never really arguments but rough conversations because I didn't feel heard or understood. I'm sure he felt the same way about me. I wanted to always have friends over, friends we had together, and family because sometimes they were my only connection to the outside world. I looked forward to family gatherings. I looked forward to adult conversation, laughter, drinking, just all around being with other people other than Jorgia or the kids. On the other hand, my husband didn't care for gatherings as much because his job required him to be around people all the time. He would always say "I'm not in the mood to entertain." "I'm Tired of talking" or "I'm just tired." I understood but I was tired too in different ways. I was physically and emotionally tired. I was tired of not having anyone to talk to, tired of not having fun, tired of dealing with Jorgia, tired of being me to be honest.

There are times I did think about driving off and never looking back. Of course, I could never leave my family, but the thought did run across my mind very quickly. Me caring for Jorgia was really taking a toll on me. I was crying myself to sleep most nights as my husband lay there snoring. I was praying that God would just not wake me up. I was having a hard time understanding what my purpose was anymore. Don't get me wrong, I loved life, but I wasn't sure if I loved mine anymore. I wanted to live but I wasn't sure if I wanted to live like this anymore. I was trying to make my husband understand the little things I wanted to do were important. It helped me forget how I was really feeling, at least for a little while. Understand though, my husband was my everything. He always went above and beyond to make me happy; I knew I was being selfish in a way because his job was not easy, he had feelings too. Even though he wasn't dealing with Jorgia the way I was, he still cared about how I was feeling. He brought me roses even when it wasn't a holiday or my birthday. He would bring me my favorite candy; he called throughout the day to see how I was doing.

My husband was my best friend, but that doesn't mean my feelings weren't valid as well. I didn't want to be insensitive to his feelings at all, I just knew I was going crazy. I would feel some kind of way because he was always going out to lunch with clients at new restaurants, trying new foods. I started saying I need to find some friends too, but he would always say, "Baby these are not my friends they are my clients." I heard him, but I still felt very left out. He would have golf tournaments that lasted all day while drinking beer and having adult conversations. To me he was having a good time while I was home living a nightmare. I just thought it was unfair to me and to him as well because it literally was his job, but I couldn't shake the fact that I was hurt because I wanted to do these things with my husband. To me, his job had robbed me of my happiness.

He would never do anything intentionally to hurt me, but I must admit I was hurting badly. It was hard to hear how his day went, but I really wanted to know because I did care and I love him, but I wish he really understood what I was going through while he was out with clients. I was probably dealing with a tantrum, Jorgia screaming or destroying our property. I can guarantee something was going on. I longed for those adult outings, I was suffering inside, and I hated myself for feeling this way. I didn't feel like myself anymore. I had lost myself and I was trying so hard to find me again. I wanted to be more than just Jorgia's care provider. I wanted to be more than just a stay-at-home mom. I wanted more out of life. I wanted to do things that made me happy or made me feel good. Sometimes we did things when we had a babysitter or things lined up to make it possible, but it just never seemed as if it was enough, or it was over too fast. I doubted if I would ever get back to being me again. I was lost and just wanted to be heard and understood, I wanted to be found, I wanted and needed help but couldn't admit that out loud.

I was trying to keep up the image of being so strong, being the best mom especially to Jorgia. Little did they know I felt like a weak shell of myself and putting up a front was easy. Being truthful was hard. I never wanted to appear weak, so I did the best I could hide and mask those feelings because I didn't want to hurt anyone, especially if what I was feeling was wrong. Just having a bad day sometimes brings up all these feelings, and bad days happen often. I felt disgusted and angry at myself because I also felt I was not being a good wife to my husband. It wasn't only because of how I felt about his job but how I felt that autism was killing my sex life. It was slowly diminishing. My sex drive was gone. I wanted to have sex, I desired my husband so much, I loved my husband more than life itself. I just didn't have the energy. I was sleep deprived which definitely didn't help, my mind was saying yes but my body was screaming no!

When I went to bed at night as soon as I lay down, sometimes I didn't even know I was asleep until Jorgia woke me up or I woke up on my own. I didn't feel sexy, I didn't feel pretty, I felt run down and my body constantly ached. I felt like I was 100 years old. I was sexually frustrated and I'm for certain my husband was too. My husband deserved so much more. He never pressured me, He never said anything, but I knew it had to be even more frustrating for him as well. I just didn't know how to fix this. I felt so broken and ready to give up.

My husband always tells me I am a great mom and wife. I want to be a better wife and mom but where do I find the strength when I have to fight a beast all day? The beast was Autism. I hated autism. Autism has destroyed my life! Why wasn't there a cure?. Why wasn't there medication to make it go away? Why can't they do brain surgery and correct whatever is wrong? The nights I wasn't sleeping these are just a few questions I would lay there crying wondering WHY?. The questions were endless and the sad part about it is that they went unanswered. It was hard to give myself to my husband because I couldn't shut my mind off. I couldn't stop thinking about how I had to do this all over the next day. How I would wake up and be forced to get up when I wasn't even awake yet. It was very difficult, and I'm ashamed to say sex was the last thing on my mind. There was no room in my mind. It was overflowing with things that was apparently out of my control. I was tired of being tired. I knew I would never take my own life as I have said before. It was a quick thought, but I was also afraid of who would care for my kids, especially Jorgia. I was all they had. No matter what, they needed me, and I had to keep pushing.

I was even afraid of just getting sick because I knew I had to still take care of her. I remember being in my husband's company car coming home one night after picking Jorgia up from the Autism center. Traffic was horrific. It was so bad that cars began to pass other cars and diesels on the right shoulder which wasn't a passing lane. The diesel was just sitting there in the middle of the road as they passed. After they passed I decided I was going to do the same thing. As soon as I began to pass the diesel decided to turn right into a fast-food parking lot and began dragging my car sideways. I was headed right into a post. I was laying on my horn screaming but there was no way he could hear me. The truck was so big it made it impossible to hear me in a little Ford Fusion. I glanced in the back seat because all I could think about was my baby girl. I quickly made a decision to hit the gas to avoid hitting the post and we landed in the middle of a deserted parking lot next to the fast-food parking lot where he was turning in.

I put the car in park and jumped out of the car. I was trying to move fast but I was moving slow. I then realized I was moving slowly because I was shaking so bad from the trauma of it all. My hands were shaking so much I could barely open the door. I was finally able to open the door and Jorgia was in the back laughing and playing like nothing happened. I was grateful to God for his protection. I phoned my husband immediately apologizing for wrecking his car. He said he didn't give a damn about that car as long as we were OK. He said this could have ended very badly and he was grateful to see his girls walk away from this. These are moments I think about. If something would have happened to me I needed to at least let my husband know what to do. It taught me to write down Jorgia's medications and dosages, and make sure life insurance policies were intact. Believe it or not these things are very important, and I wanted no regrets. It really opens your eyes and makes you look at things a lot differently.

When Jorgia was about seven years old I injured myself while shopping at Walmart. This incident made me realize how consumed I was with Jorgia. I was planning on having a little girl's night with my God-Grandchildren. We stopped at Walmart to get some snacks for movie time. I was trotting to the counter to pay for the snacks. As I got close to the counter I noticed there was an ice cream machine by the checkout leaking water. As soon as I stepped in front of the machine I slipped and on the way down I somehow twisted my body. When I hit the floor I heard my back crack. I was in excruciating pain; all I could do was scream and cry as I laid on the floor. I couldn't move at all. I heard someone say, "Don't move her until the ambulance gets here." The snacks were all over the place along with my shoes. I was totally embarrassed. I couldn't believe this just happened. They immediately called for an ambulance that arrived pretty quickly. Right before the EMT's arrived the manager of Walmart made me move onto an electric cart. When I tried to step upon the cart it moved forward because it wasn't shut off. I jerked so hard I eventually learned I got whiplash from that incident.

When I finally got into the ambulance they checked me out and recommended I go to the hospital for x-rays. I made a decision that later hurt me in regard to the lawsuit. I decided not to go to the hospital, I went home because I knew Jorgia was on a schedule and was used to doing things a certain way. I didn't want her to end up having a bad night because I wasn't there, so I decided to go home and go to the hospital the next day. Everything I did and every decision I made was always made with Jorgia in mind.

After seeing the doctor, I was told I had a lumbar sprain in my back, bruised wrist, bruised hip, and whiplash. I was sore and stiff for a couple of weeks. Even though I was in pain my life didn't stop, it didn't even slow down. Jorgia would hardly let anyone else help her besides me. She wanted me because that's what she was used to. I was moving slowly doing my best, but it was like pins and needles poking me all over my back with every step I took. I had stabbing pains shooting down my back through my legs. I was crying as I continued to do what I needed to do. My husband and kids would help as much as possible, but I think the goal was not to upset Jorgia because it would make everything worse. I hated when I was sick because it really intensified everything in my life. I slept downstairs for a while because going up and down the stairs was very painful. I did have to go upstairs when I needed to take her to bed and that was unbearable to say the least, but I had no choice.

I knew deep down inside our lives were very different from most people's lives. I tried to continue to do normal family things especially during holidays, which were the best times of the year. Having family and friends over, having a few drinks, eating, talking, and laughing. It was always short lived for me because I still had to make sure Jorgia was OK. In her own way she would manage to create an uncomfortable situation. It would be so embarrassing when Jorgia was trying to attack the children that were playing. She would even start screaming and trying to throw things. I know our family and friends always said they understood and not to feel embarrassed, but I just couldn't help it. I couldn't help but wonder if they just didn't want to say how they really felt and what they were saying behind my back. To be honest I probably would do exactly what I thought they were doing. Not so much as talk about them but discuss how hard it must be and wishing I could do more to help. I didn't want sympathy but what else could you do when your child is raging out of control but be embarrassed? I tried to keep smiling, and tried everything I could to calm her down, but as usual nothing was working. Once again It was out of my control.

During Thanksgiving one year my husband's family was with us, and we had the music going, cooking, and having a great time. Jorgia went into a severe meltdown. I took a deep breath knowing where this was about to go. I recognized every sign, and I knew things were about to take a turn for the worse. My husband's sister's Steffani and Laverne tried to step in and help because I had my hands full cooking, but Jorgia began attacking them and throwing things off the table that was next to her. I knew I had to get over to her quickly. They had no idea what she really was capable of. I was so hurt and ashamed. I knew I shouldn't be, but it was hard not to feel that way especially when I just couldn't get control of her or the situation. When I went over to her then she would start to attack me in front of everyone. I just dropped my head in shame. This is when I start regretting having holiday gatherings because they would turn into a holiday nightmare. I was Jorgia's mom and in moments like these I felt like a complete stranger to my daughter. It would chip off another piece of my heart. I would eventually be able to have a little bit of fun once Jorgia went to bed. I didn't always want to wait until she went to bed, but I had no choice. I was grateful that at least she went to bed every night at the same time no matter what. I must say that was the best thing about our routine.

Now since being on the new medication she was even starting to sleep all night. I waited years for that to happen. Granted, we still have our occasional middle-of-the-night wake ups, but it's definitely gotten better. I think God finally showed me a little mercy. There were times during a party or gathering I would sometimes have to leave to go put her to bed. I hated leaving the party or conversations but when she was ready to go to bed I had to take her before she got upset. Her medication would make her drowsy around bedtime. I would take her upstairs and I could hear the party going on and everyone laughing. I hated the feeling of missing out on things. I didn't get many moments to enjoy company, so it made it hard to leave.

What was heartbreaking was when Jorgia had birthdays and there really weren't any friends to invite. I did my best to invite friends and family of ours who were happy to come and bring her gifts, but she just didn't like all the commotion. She did not do well around a large gathering of people. This was called sensory overload which made it difficult to celebrate special days for her or any holiday for that matter. She never really even understood gifts. She would get toys and things but only played with them a short time before she would become totally uninterested. I remember several birthdays and Christmases. I would spend so much time on what to get her and it would crush me to see her not even want it. I recall buying her one of those big electric cars that you had to get in and push the gas to drive, I had also bought her a bike. She didn't know how to drive the car, it just kept bumping into things because she had no clue how to control it with the steering wheel. She didn't even know how to pedal to make the bike go. I had to return both of those items. These are moments as a mom I just wanted to break down, this wasn't normal and could never get used to this. I was used to my other kids and how they always reacted to things, so this was definitely out of the ordinary.

I remember for her 10th birthday I heard about a place in the mall called Build a Bear and they had birthday parties. I thought this was perfect, so I immediately started planning. My goddaughter Leona and her children came, Jorgia's brothers Garyn, Garrison, Shamari and sister Shana and a few cousins were there. They got to build their own personal bear by choosing the bear they wanted and stuffing it themselves. They also got to choose to dress the bear in any outfit in the store. Jorgia seemed to be enjoying herself except for a few moments she started to get a little impatient. Of course, I was on edge and nervous hoping she stayed calm and this all would go well. I always wanted the best for her. I wanted to treat her as normal as possible but sometimes her reaction and her actions make me second guess myself constantly. I was never at ease, I was always scared and waiting for her to explode.

Surprisingly, she did pretty well. We got through the party after everyone dressed their bears, took a couple of photos, and got ready to head to the other end of the mall to have some food and hopefully some cake. We all got there and sat down, and Jorgia began to cry and say, "Ready to go " several times. I knew what that meant, so now I was sweating with panic because I was trying to calm her down. I wasn't ready for the party to end. I wanted to hang out and eat and have a conversation with one of my old girlfriends who showed up. I was happy to see her and my aunt as well. Jorgia just wouldn't relax. She seemed to be getting more and more upset. I looked at my husband with sadness as he was also enjoying himself with the kids. I said, "We have to go." He knew exactly what I meant.

It was so frustrating to have to leave the party and my boys had to leave as well. They were not ready to go. I had planned this party and invited everyone and now I had to leave them all behind. Some family and friends would tell me just to ignore her she would be fine and not to leave but they didn't understand how ugly it could get. My husband offered to take her home and let me stay, as he always considers my feelings, but I knew she would give him a hard time. It's not that I didn't think he could handle it, I just didn't like seeing her get that upset.

We said goodbye to everyone with such a heavy heart as we exited the mall with laughter in the background. I was going home to nothing. I felt angry, and I started to have those thoughts in my head again "Why Me? Damn, this sucks." I loved Jorgia but moments like this made me hate autism. I think I was subconsciously mad at her too. Why couldn't she just play with the other kids and why couldn't she just be normal? It was hard to be happy for the little victories like her lasting at least through the party. I was being selfish and complaining about the things I couldn't do. I wanted to be grateful, but I was so tired of always having to cut things short or always being on edge because of what she might do.

Chapter 17

I often wondered if my husband felt a little cheated by having a daughter with autism. I have asked him before and he would always say, no and that she is here for a reason, and that he loves her. I understood his answers, but when I would see him talking with our goddaughter and granddaughters and how he interacted with them it warmed my heart. He would sometimes say things like "Little girls are so funny." and "Little girls are such a blessing." He loved to converse with them because they had no filter. They would say things that made you laugh so hard. So, I know deep down inside he does feel a little cheated or some kind of way, but he will never admit it. I have always felt like I failed him for not giving him that little girl he yearned for just as much as I did.

One day My god-granddaughters came over to spend the weekend and they loved Jorgia. That day, we decided to get out of the house and go window shopping knowing I would probably be spending some money because I loved spoiling them. My husband and I got Jorgia's wheelchair, packed the girls into the car and went to an indoor swap meet. Jorgia was not having it, she wanted to leave after about ten minutes in the store. We constantly tried to do things to keep her mind off of leaving. The girls didn't want to leave. I was being tugged in many directions. I didn't know if we should leave or stay.

My husband was pushing Jorgia around the store trying to keep her busy and trying to get attention on something she might like, but nothing was working.

I could hear her crying from across the store. I then told my husband to take her to the car while we checked out. Once again we were going to have to leave. The girls just didn't want to go home and now Jorgia was calm again, so we decided to try one more store. We went to another store called 5 Below. The girls were so excited, they wanted everything they saw. This is the type of quality time I would give my life to spend with my own daughter, but I knew that would never happen. We went inside the store and unfortunately Jorgia started doing the same thing. My husband took her to the car and gave the girls ten minutes to look around the store and we were going to have to leave. They were sad but understood. Jorgia just didn't like being out in public and this was so far from how she used to be. The older she got the more she just wanted to be home.

Time was really flying; the years were passing so quickly I didn't realize my baby girl was about to enter junior high school. I was always afraid of her getting older but unfortunately we were here. I was excited too because I was looking forward to having more time for myself. Jorgia would start spending more time at school and the autism center. This means she would be gone basically all day and when she came home it would soon be time for bed. I was so elated I didn't know what to do with myself. It had been me and her for a long time and I also wasn't sure how she was going to react to such a grueling schedule. I would still take her and pick her up from school.

I was making plans to maybe go back to school online, and to start focusing more on things I enjoyed, but in baby steps, one thing at a time. This was going to be the best year I have had since our vow renewal which was the best day of my life as well as giving birth to my children. I loved my family. No words could describe how I felt. I was also looking forward to our 18th wedding anniversary which was right around the corner. Eighteen years with my husband was one of the best accomplishments in my entire life and one of the best decisions I ever made. My husband was planning a big getaway, and I just couldn't stop smiling. Even Jorgia couldn't take my happiness away.

My husband was taking me up to Yosemite to a cabin for the weekend where we would enjoy a tour, eating, enjoying the outdoors, and all-round fresh air that I longed for. I was on top of the world. I was booking the cabin, I was researching online schools, also getting Jorgia prepared for her big year too. Seventh grade was a big deal. Being diagnosed with Cystic Fibrosis we didn't know how bad it would be or if she would even be here, so it was truly a blessing for us to see her reach such major milestones.

During vacation or holidays, it was very hard with Jorgia being home all day. She was used to a certain schedule or routine and whenever that was interrupted she was not happy, and we all felt her wrath. Although we enjoyed being home and my husband loved having time off she made being home miserable in every way. We couldn't watch television because it was hard to hear what they were saying over her screaming. We would try different things the therapists suggested but she was very stubborn and very strong willed. Everything we tried was an epic fail.

She would have tantrums so bad that eventually I had to restrain her in her wheelchair so she would stop destroying things and hurting other people including me and herself. It was impossible to settle down and relax. We truly missed days that we could relax at home and enjoy a good movie. Now we had to wait until she went to bed just to watch TV, and by that time we were so beat up we probably would fall asleep before it started. Times like this made me wish I had brothers or sisters that I could call on to help me. Maybe they could have taken her for the day or even the weekend, but I just didn't have that in my life.

I would often get invited to events, such as weddings, birthday parties, even just get-togethers that I had to turn down because I couldn't bring Jorgia along or find a babysitter. After a while I stopped receiving invites. Some people didn't understand even when I told them why. I think they felt as if I was making excuses, but they had no idea what I was dealing with. I knew no one would understand, and there was no way they could. I didn't even have the energy or the words to begin to explain. They knew Jorgia was autistic, but they had no clue about the monster we were living with behind closed doors. It was almost like we were living a secret life. When we were home with Jorgia it felt like we were locked in a cage with her and under her mercy. She was in full control. We were clueless while trying to figure out how to survive Jorgia. When we had company or when we were around people we made it seem as if we had control, but Jorgia eventually made us look lost and confused. The truth came out every time very quickly because she was so unpredictable. You just couldn't figure her out.

There were family members that never bothered to check on us to see if we needed help or just to ask how we were doing except my aunties who were like mothers to me and my older children. They always tried to help in any way but even they still didn't really understand the whole truth of what we were up against daily. They had their own lives which made it difficult to extend a hand to help me. I totally understood but it would have been nice to have that extended family to just help relieve that stress or give me a break when I felt like I was going to break. Jorgia was a challenge I wasn't ready for. I had to learn as I went, and I had to get it wrong many times before I got it right.

The therapist would give us advice to try and help us have more peaceful days at home. They would tell us things like ignore her, don't give in to her, let her do more things herself that they knew she could, because when we would do things for her it would feed into her bad behavior. I understood what they were saying but it was the hardest thing to do because we gave into her a lot just to quiet the tantrums or just to get that moment of quietness. It didn't last long, but we took what we could get. We never gave up, we would still try to do family things, or take her out on outings. We were really trying hard not to become prisoners to autism.

I used to love taking Jorgia to my son's football games to see him play. Of course, I would miss a couple of plays thanks to her needing or wanting something. It became so demanding taking her to games especially when it would be windy. I had to remember to keep her warm as possible to keep her Cystic Fibrosis from becoming a problem. I did my best to protect her but even that was taxing. It was a lot of work taking her out in public. There was just always something to worry about which made it hard to concentrate, or just have fun. It was better sometimes to just stay home. Even though it was tough for me to go places or travel, my husband still had to do what he had to do when it came to his job.

The end of January 2019 right after my birthday, my husband was returning from one of his company trips from Florida. I couldn't get to the airport quick enough. I don't like being away from my husband. He makes me feel so deeply loved, I feel so safe when he's home. He makes me feel special every day and he always treats me like a queen. I always felt so undeserving especially knowing the feelings I was carrying in my heart about the things he was able to do that I couldn't. When I saw him coming out of the airport I hugged him so tight and never wanted to let go. Those four days seemed like a lifetime. I was happy he was home but this particular time he didn't seem like himself.

He kept saying he wasn't feeling well and needed to just lay down. On the ride home he was also telling me how the news about the great Kobe Bryant, an NBA Legend's death, flashed across every TV screen in the airport. He talked about how horrible the helicopter crash was and how our country was in disbelief. When we arrived home he went straight to bed which was very unusual for my husband. He rarely got sick, he never missed work either. I didn't know what was going on. I figured maybe he just needed to sleep it off. He slept all day and got worse as time passed. He was sounding a little congested and had no appetite. I was trying to keep my distance as well as keep the kids away from him because I didn't know what he had. I was especially worried about Jorgia I really had to protect her from getting sick. That was the last thing I needed.

I continued to care for him the best way I could. I made him soup and checked in on him periodically. He stated that he also felt dizzy at times. For the next few days, my husband slept basically all day, eating very little and absolutely no energy. After about three to four days, he started to feel somewhat better and tried to get back to himself. Within a couple of weeks, we started to hear news reports about a virus going around called COVID. We had a feeling that's probably what he had when he returned from Florida.

We didn't know what was going on. Schools started closing, stores were shutting down and the whole world started going on lock down. The virus was spreading rapidly, the world was in a state of panic. They were reporting that this virus was hitting people with underlying health issues worse. We listened closely to the news daily trying to keep updated. I have never been so afraid in my life. Thousands of people were dying without loved ones being to say goodbye. Our country was in bad shape. I was concerned for my family, especially Jorgia, if this virus hit her. It would be devastating. My mind was racing. My kids were so afraid the world outside was literally dark, the streets were quiet. People were stocking up on food so much there was hardly anything left, prices went through the roof because we need to survive, and businesses took advantage of us in a very vulnerable state. ·

The kids were home every day due to the schools being closed. They were working hard to figure out an on-line education plan for the kids. Since this was all new it was going to take time and strategy to make sure every student was receiving what they needed to continue their education during this horrific tragedy. We were clueless as to what was going to happen and how this would end. The death toll was climbing every day. People were scared to go outside or be around anyone. The whole entire world became prisoners in their own homes. This wasn't anything new to me. I had trained many years for this situation. The only difference is the whole family was here with me.

Jorgia didn't understand why she couldn't go to school or the Autism center.

She started to act out because her routine was interrupted, and it had completely stopped. I couldn't talk to her to make her understand what was happening, all I could say was "no school yet, no center yet." She would cry and cream. She constantly repeated one the therapist names daily. She would say Cindy over and over and over. She had been doing this already for a while, but it got worse during the lock down. She would call my name and when I would answer her she would just say "Cindy." She pretty much did everyone that way. It became the most annoying thing ever. If you ignored her she would get louder that would then send her into a tantrum the more you ignored the behavior. We thought we were miserable before this, but this was beyond miserable and there was nothing we could do. I was at my wit's end. This was catastrophic to the entire world.

I started researching again to see if there was anything I could use or do to help calm her down a little. We were all searching for some sort of peace. I ran across a video of a mother talking about using CBD oils that helped calm her daughter who suffered from autism and seizures. In the video the little girl was having a seizure and began screaming. The mother gave her the CBD oil and you can actually see her start to calm down within minutes. I thought this is it! How can I get some? Where do I go? I first tried to go through her doctor to see if they can refer her to someone that can prescribe it or recommend something that I could try. However, there was a CBD doctor that did not accept insurance and required a $700 first visit payment. I did not have that kind of money, so I proceeded to research buying it on my own.

I googled several stores and spoke to several people. I asked many questions regarding the oils. I do remember a few years back my husband brought home some CBD brownies and I gave Jorgia a bite and she ended up having diarrhea, so I didn't want to repeat that situation. I was very careful and decided to try a very low dose of gummies and oils. Sometimes it seemed to work and other times it didn't seem to not affect her at all. We eventually moved the dosage up a little at a time but she hated the taste of the gummies so she wouldn't eat them. It all was a failure. I just stopped all together. Jorgia was a hard nut to crack. What worked for everyone else just didn't work for her. I thought maybe she is just stubborn and fighting against everything we do. She was very strong minded as well which was a bad combination.

We were months in, and the lock down was still going on, death was all around. The virus was hitting every city and state. There was nowhere to go. Jorgia had no school or therapy in person; mostly it was all online. She wanted no parts of it. She half paid attention; she didn't understand the concept, so her attention span was all over the place. She would even fall asleep during some of her sessions. I had my other son homeschooling as well and I had other things I had to do as a wife and mom. My house was hectic.

Jorgia did not like to see me sit down or rest. She watched my every move. Most days I had to try and stay busy by cleaning up, doing laundry, sweeping, mopping, putting away clothes, doing dishes, paying bills and the list goes on. As long as I didn't sit down she was fine. I would try to sneak to the couch and sit down and she would immediately ask for food or apple juice. I would have to stop Jorgia because she would make herself sick from overeating just to annoy me or bother me. She would drink a whole carton of Capri Sun juice packets within 1 to 2 hours. We would hide out in other rooms just so she wouldn't bother us. It was so uncomfortable, and I felt bad staying away from her, but I just needed to sit down for a moment. It was exhausting catering to Jorgia.

It was extremely overwhelming. I would step outside to get some fresh air and she would purposely go to the potty, so I had to come in and see about her. Jorgia was sometimes too smart for her own good. She knew how to get me back in the house. If I didn't come fast enough, she would totally destroy the bathroom. She would get into lotion, toothpaste, rip up toilet paper all over the bathroom. Her tantrums would consist of trying to pull down curtains, throwing TV remotes, screaming to the top of her lungs, scratching, pinching, biting, and making this high pitch squealing sound I had never heard before. This sound could probably bust your eardrums. I don't know how she was doing it. It's almost sounds like she was sucking in air and doing a high-pitched whistle at the same time. It was the most annoying sound. I would walk around the house with her headphones on trying to muffle as much of the sound as possible. This was something else to add to the list of things I had to live with when it came to Jorgia.

My depression was growing daily. I wanted to just sleep knowing I wouldn't have to deal with her. I walked slowly with no urgency at all, I never smiled, I wasn't eating much. I had to pull energy from somewhere to just get through each day, even my reserve energy was all depleted. I was empty! I just felt I had nothing to live for. I was Jorgia's personal butler, maid, cook, nurse, punching bag... oh yeah and her mom. It almost started to seem as if she hated me because I was her main target, her number one target when she was mad. It was even hard to eat during the day. My husband and I would sneak and eat in another room and my son would eat in his room. We were all trying to avoid Jorgia. It didn't matter if she had just eaten or not. She would want what you had which meant give it to her and make some more or the wrath of Jorgia was coming.

She was like a tornado of emotions she couldn't understand or control on her own, which always lead to an in-home disaster. I learned to wait and cook dinner once she went to bed because we wanted to all eat in peace. This was very sad because we would have loved to have Jorgia eat with us as a family and spend quality time with her whenever we had an opportunity. But Jorgia was not making things like that easy so we had to make tough decisions to exclude her so we could manage to stay sane.

Once she started sleeping all night, I started living for her bedtime. I watched the clock every day waiting for 6pm. That's the time she took her night meds and was ready for bed by 7pm. Sadly that was the highlight of my day every day because being stuck in this house with Jorgia daily was driving me crazy. I knew that would be the only time I could actually sit down and rest, watch TV, and be able to hear what they were saying. I looked forward to actually, finishing my food or snack without having to give it up. I was able to just simply have some peace and quiet. I started not even wanting to go to sleep because I was scared of the next day coming so fast and having to start all over. I would stay up as late as I could and end up having to suffer the consequences of that the next day. Sometimes it was worth it. The challenges of raising and caring for Jorgia made my daily life a living hell.

During the day I would have to just take a minute to go upstairs and lay on my bed and just cry. I was exhausted to the point that my legs and feet were throbbing and hurting so bad from getting up and down all day. I was over this COVID situation. I needed these kids out of the house and back in school. This virus came at the wrong time, just when everything was seemingly starting to get better.

I was in total disbelief that this was going on in the world right now! There is a deadly virus that has shut down the entire world and then there is Jorgia who has our home in utter chaos. I knew I was going to go crazy sooner or later, I was on the edge of losing my mind. Some days she just didn't show up for online school because I just didn't even have the energy to sit in front of a computer. I didn't even have the energy to explain to the teachers I was tired. I didn't care anymore, I was done! I am so ashamed to admit there were days I didn't shower because my strength had drained out completely. I felt so dead inside.

This virus was not going anywhere any time soon, we were trying to move toward a way to get back to our lives. They started opening things back up but with major restrictions. Only a certain number of people were allowed in the stores at a time, and even then you had to wear a mask or face shields. People were sanitizing and washing their hands more than ever. We were living in fear. I was so nervous and afraid of Jorgia catching COVID, if she did I had no idea what would happen.

Jorgia spent the whole 7th grade basically at home homeschooling and the first part of 8th grade due to this virus. During her eighth-grade year they began to open the schools back up for the ones that wanted to start coming back to in person schooling. Coming back would require certain stipulations like wearing a mask, and checking temperatures at the gate before kids could come in. No one else including parents were allowed in the school. Although I couldn't wait to get Jorgia out of the house, I knew this virus was still impacting our country and I didn't want to put her in a situation that would cause her to catch this deadly virus. I knew it would be challenging just to get her to wear a mask. Oh my god, this was just another obstacle to attack with Jorgia. If I wanted her back in school this had to be accomplished.

Her therapy was back in person as well, but only at home and the therapist had to stay masked up. I was able to take advantage of them being there, by having that little moment to gather myself, just to go outside and breathe. While they were there the therapist worked on Jorgia wearing her mask and keeping it on for small periods at a time and increasing the time more and more until she was used to wearing her mask. She was continuing homeschooling until I felt comfortable with her going back in person and I was also waiting for her doctor to release her as well.

Through the news we started hearing about the COVID vaccine that would protect you from COVID. It didn't protect you from getting COVID, it would only protect you if you got the virus, you would not get it as bad. When we heard back from her doctor she recommended we all get vaccinated before releasing Jorgia back to school. Getting her vaccinated was going to be hell. I knew I had to do it knowing I needed to protect her as much as possible. This was a new vaccine which made it even more scary. The things you hear in the news about taking this vaccine made you not want to take a chance on it. At the same time, I had to trust God, the same god I had been angry with all these years, the same god that I thought hated me all these years. He was the same god I knew would never leave me nor forsake me. I had no choice. I had to trust in him and pray for my daughter's protection. I had to also have faith and believe the vaccine would be safe for her. After much convincing from her doctor and many discussions between my husband and I we decided to go get vaccinated as a family. We had to stick together, good, or bad.

I went online and scheduled vaccinations for Jorgia, My husband, my son, and myself. I was a little concerned how she would do with getting vaccinated, but we had to get it done. I was hoping and praying there would be no side effects. We went in that next week to Walgreens to get our COVID shot. The vaccine had to be done in 3 doses. We were getting the first one which had minimal side effects like tiredness or just a sore arm, but everyone reacts differently. We had to choose between the Pfizer, Moderna, or Jonson and Johnson vaccine. We chose Pfizer. When we got there I must say it was pretty crowded which made me very nervous because I didn't know how she was going to react or how long I could keep her calm.

My husband was pushing her around the store while I did registration paperwork. Then we had to wait. It was taking a while and Jorgia was getting very anxious and was starting to cry and started asking to go home. I was praying they would hurry up because I needed to get this done and did not want to have to reschedule. After about 20 minutes they called our name. I wanted her to go first to get it out the way. I sat her in my lap with her back to me. Jorgia was watching very closely; I think she knew what was about to happen because as soon as the pharmacist stuck the needle in she jerked so hard it caught me off guard. He removed the needle very quickly. It didn't hurt her, but it just scared us to death. She cried a little, but she did well for what it was. We all finished up and went home. Jorgia was fine, her arm was probably a little sore because ours was as well. My husband and I were tired but nothing unusual. Now that she was vaccinated or at least started the process I felt better sending her back to school. She was also doing much better with the mask. Once she starts seeing the other kids with masks knowing she is not the only one I think she would be fine.

A week after receiving the vaccination Jorgia got a little stuffy as she sometimes does. I thought nothing of it. Then I started noticing she was laying around more than usual. I heard my son Garrison saying he couldn't taste or smell anything as well. I had a feeling, for once, that I knew what was going on. I didn't want to believe it, but I was 99% sure because they were having COVID symptoms. They were giving out COVID tests everywhere because the virus was going strong. The world looked so much different from what we were used to. We never knew what people's faces even looked like anymore, we forgot what hugs felt like, we missed seeing and being around friends and family. We were so fed up with this freaking COVID. I was going to be pissed if my daughter tested positive.

I made an appointment with premium urgent care for the whole family to get tested and get results within an hour. The test was very uncomfortable by sticking that Q-tip down one side of your nose, it felt like they touched your brain. It makes you sneeze uncontrollably. We all got through it, but it was very unpleasant. Before we could get home. I received the emails with all of our test results. I was shaking like a leaf from a tree on a windy day. I wanted to know, but I didn't want to know. I clicked on the first email which was my son Garrison as the page came up. The first thing I saw was Positive, my heart dropped, and I started shaking even more, I felt my body heating up and beginning to sweat. The moment I was dreading but I needed to know. I clicked on Jorgia's name and the page began to load. All of a sudden Positive was staring me straight in my face. My husband Gary was positive too. I was the only one that received a negative test. This was the most daunting thing I have experienced.

What the hell was I supposed to do now? I have to try and take care of everyone and at the same time try to protect myself from catching this virus. I had to also start Jorgia on her breathing treatments to make sure the virus didn't aggravate her Cystic Fibrosis. This was one of the longest and scariest weeks of my life, it was complete terror. I was scared and felt depleted. I was worrying myself sick watching Jorgia so closely praying and hoping she didn't get worse. If God didn't hate me this would be a great time to prove it to me… "Just let my family pull through this and be OK." It was so hard to have faith or be positive when you hear the unthinkable on TV all day. Constant news of how people were slipping into comas, and not recovering, they were dying, they couldn't breathe. The ones with health issues were not making it through. This was by far the most tragically terrorizing event I had ever seen in my lifetime. I was in total dismay, but I couldn't give up on my family. They need me more than they ever had. I refused to let them down. I thought for sure it was the end of time I heard about growing up in church. It sure felt like it.

I continued to do the best I could day by day, barely sleeping, barely having time to eat. I felt so lonely, so weak. I was making sure everyone was taking their meds on schedule, I was feeding everyone when they were hungry. I was proud of myself for staying strong and doing what I had to do nursing my family back to health. They were in quarantine for 14 days. I can say with great pride I survived hell week, and my family came through with flying colors. God never left my side. He gave me the strength I needed to be there for my family, and I truly felt blessed, and I couldn't thank God enough for watching over us. I had been wrong about God, he has never left me, he was there all along. I needed to trust him more.

Thanks to this devastating virus Jorgia had missed out on seventh grade so this was my first time driving her to this school for the rest of her eighth-grade year. It was so far from where we lived. It was at least 15 to 20 minutes away depending on traffic. I could tell Jorgia was excited and happy to be going back to school. She was laughing and seemed happy on the drive. I knew things would look very different for her with wearing a mask and being at a new school. She had only seen her teachers through FaceTime so this would be the first time she would see them in person. I was worried about leaving her, but I definitely needed the break, so I had mixed feelings of excitement and worry.

Chapter 18

We started to get back into a somewhat normal routine with Jorgia being back at school and having therapy at home after school. I was picking my son up from school after picking Jorgia up every day because his school was on the way home. It was perfect. After a couple of weeks my husband decided to transfer my son to another school that was across town because of football opportunities which meant I now had to pick him up after Jorgia and this made for even longer drives after school every day.

Jorgia was so used to being home every day I was concerned about how she was going to react being back at school especially being in a whole other environment. She was experiencing a Different school, different teachers, longer drives, wearing masks, and this was all new for her. I didn't know what to expect. The drives with Jorgia started to become very intense, she started becoming very impatient and angry, more after school rather than before. When I would pick her up before my son transferred to the new school she would do OK until we got about halfway to the school or at a certain point on the drive. She would start with that very high screeching noise and that always let me know she was about to tantrum. She would then start banging on the window so hard I thought it was going to break. I tried rolling down the window, but she would then start trying to throw things out the window, so I had to roll it back up quickly. Jorgia would then begin screaming so loud my head would start hurting and ears were ringing. I tried hard to ignore her and focus on the road, but it just made her angrier. She was reaching through the middle of the front seat trying to scratch me and trying to pull my hair. I had to scoot close as I could to the steering wheel to keep her from reaching me. Just when I thought it couldn't get any worse she started kicking the seat as hard as she could while still screaming. I was driving very uncomfortably while trying to keep from wrecking and trying to keep my eyes on Jorgia because I didn't know what she would do next. I felt the tears coming as my heart felt like it stopped beating. My chest was hurting from holding my breath trying not to cry.

We were almost at my son's school as traffic began to get a little backed up. My intensity was through the roof, I just wanted her out of the car. I wanted to get home as quickly as possible. I texted my son Garrison who knew exactly how Jorgia was. I said "Son, as soon as the bell rings hurry because I have Jorgia with me," he replied back, "OK, mom." I had to park and wait for my son as Jorgia was still in full blown tantrum mode. I was embarrassed as other parents parked next to me could hear the screams. I had to get out of the car and get into the backseat with her and try to calm her down.

She tried to attack me at first, but I never gave up. I felt like we were putting on a show as parents and kids walking by were probably wondering what was going on. Once again I felt so embarrassed. I was upset at Jorgia for doing this to me. I couldn't express my anger towards her because she had no clue what she was doing let alone how I felt. I couldn't punish her or scold her. I had to just take it. These moments I just didn't feel like her mom.

I just couldn't help how I felt. I wondered what people really thought and if I would feel the same way. I think I would. We never understand anyone's situation, so this has definitely taught me to stop judging people and maybe offer some assistance. It's OK to ask if someone may need help. People were just used to overlooking autistic kids. They didn't matter and didn't have time for them. It wasn't their problem, so they never wanted to get involved. I don't blame them at all.

My son finally reached the car, and we hurried home as the tantrum started back up immediately as we began to drive off. Luckily, we were about five minutes from home but with Jorgia it felt like an hour. Getting home was never the end of tantrums. They would sometimes still happen on and off through the day, we just didn't know how bad they would be until they happened. These tantrums in the car went on every day after school for weeks, which turned into months.

My husband then decided to transfer Garrison across town to another school because not only academically it would be better for him but also more opportunities for his football career. I was happy for him and only wanted the best, but I knew I was in for the ride of my life with Jorgia. When I picked her up at 2:15 pm I would have to hit the freeway to get to him, which was extremely crowded with after school traffic. When I got to his school it would be about 2:40pm. He got out at 2:55pm, by the time he got to the car it would be about 3:05pm. Now we had to head home. When we reached the house it would be about 3:30pm. Jorgia has been in the car for over an hour. This was my schedule every day. The rides from her school to his school felt like it aged me about 10 years. I have never experienced something that literally made me not only want to pull my hair out but made me want to run away from it all. I'd had enough, I couldn't do this anymore, I was feeling so alone and just didn't know what to do anymore. I threw my hands in the air, I didn't even want to try anymore.

There were definitely unforgettable moments but the one that keeps coming up for me is the one day I had picked Jorgia up from school. We headed to my son's school to pick him up. I was watching Jorgia through the rear-view mirror praying we would have a pleasant ride. I was clenching the wheel so tight as my chest felt like it was about to cave in. I was waiting for the beast to rage, my body was so tense it was like a burning sensation slowly moving from the crown of my head to the sole of my feet. I hurt all over. As soon as I heard that familiar screeching sound I knew the storm was raging. I started saying Jesus, Jesus, Jesus, Jesus praying God would take control because I had a long drive ahead of me and she was just beginning. Jorgia started her usual screaming, hitting my window nonstop with the palm of her hand, every hit was sending vibrations throughout the car. I knew my window was going to eventually break one of these times. She was getting out of her seat belt trying to attack me as I entered the freeway. I had to try and pull over on the freeway and get out of the car as cars were passing me at top speed as the wind was shaking my car.

I was seriously afraid for my life. I didn't know if someone would side swipe me, killing us both. I had to make it to the back door to try and strap her back in her seat belt as I could feel the cars so close. I was absolutely petrified. I quickly jumped in the back seat and slammed the door trying to avoid oncoming traffic and diesels. I strapped her in, but she still refused to calm down. I had to get back out of the car praying I would safely make it back to my seat. I managed to get back to the driver's seat as I proceeded back in traffic trying to make it to my son's school.

I continued driving as Jorgia continued to tantrum. She screamed and cried the whole ride. As I drove with one hand on the steering wheel as my arm with my elbow resting on the side door with my head in my hands as tears poured down my face, I thought after several rides like this I had to do something. I felt I was risking her and my life and one day this may not end very well. I was trying to figure out what my next move would be. I pulled up at Garrison's school as he approached the car to get in and he could hear her screaming, hoping none of the kids could hear, I was feeling embarrassed for him. I felt bad that he had to experience this. He was such an awesome young man; he understood but I was hurting for him. He got in the back seat to try and help calm her down, but she began to attack him, so he climbed into the front seat to get away from her.

This was unlike anything I had ever seen or been through. When I got home I thought to myself I need to put my fear to the side and put Jorgia on the school bus. The next day I made the phone call to discuss this with her teacher and she said she would speak to transportation to see if they could fit her into the route. I was scared but relieved at the same time. We both needed the change because the car rides were definitely becoming a dangerous situation. Within a week a meeting was scheduled to talk about her riding the bus. I agreed only on one condition upon her riding the bus. I wanted an aide to ride with her because of her violent tantrums. I was concerned for her safety as well as the other students. They agreed that it was a great idea and had no problem making that arrangement.

That next week the aide had to park her car at my house and ride the bus to school with Jorgia every day. I didn't have to worry about her being in the car anymore. I was able to pick up my son and not have to worry about rushing him or him being embarrassed. I was also able to take advantage of that quality time with him on the way home. I was able to ask how his day went and have a conversation with him without the horrible screams and tantrums. It was necessary change, and it was a great feeling. By the time I made it home with him, Jorgia's bus would be dropping her off right after. It worked out perfectly and everyone was safe.

I admit I did have my doubts and worries about how she would behave, but Jorgia did amazing, she loved the bus. I kind of felt some sort of way because I loved taking my daughter to school and picking her up but apparently she wasn't enjoying the rides anymore. I missed our time together. It was very important to me to see her off safely every day. However, I was always excited to see her walking out of the school after missing her all day. I had to let all those feelings go knowing I was doing what was best for her in the long run. This was teaching her a little more independence.

Through the years Jorgia had pretty good teachers with the exception of a few that would get my blood boiling. Every teacher she had understood under the doctor's orders, she was not to go outside when it's windy or cold especially without her coat or beanie cap due to her Cystic Fibrosis. Every school she attended had this written in her IEP plan which is a plan for her academics and behavior. We had IEP meetings every year to go over her plan for that upcoming year and were able to add things or take things away if needed, depending on her achievements so far. Some teachers however would do what they wanted to do, and I didn't mind calling them out on it. This was my daughter and if she got sick I was the one that had to care for her, so I had no problem speaking up when I needed to.

One day I had to pick Jorgia up early from school for a doctor's appointment. I did not inform her teacher that I was coming. This was a very windy day so Jorgia should not have been outside. I pulled into the parking lot and as I was parking I looked over and saw Jorgia coming out of the bathroom with no sweater or jacket on. She also had no beanie cap, and the wind was blowing so hard she could hardly walk. I was steaming, I was furious, I couldn't wait to let this teacher have it. I was beyond pissed! I sat in the car and texted her "Why was Jorgia outside without a jacket"? She texted back "She had to use the bathroom." I told her I understood that and that's fine, but she needed to put on a jacket and beanie whenever she had to go outside. What she texted back fueled my fire. She said, "If you want, maybe you should call the district and tell them to build us a bathroom in the class!" I saw RED again! She had me so angry I couldn't text back fast enough telling her I didn't need a bathroom built. I needed her to follow instructions regarding my daughter's health and that I didn't appreciate her going around the fact that she wasn't honoring my wishes or following a doctor's orders. This teacher was one of those teachers that didn't like being wrong, she had an excuse for everything. She also claimed Jorgia was in a hurry and it would have taken too much time to put on her jacket and beanie cap. With every excuse I felt the blood racing to my head, I was getting angrier and angrier with every reply. I just began ignoring her text.

This situation made me so furious I called the district superintendent that I had spoken to several times, so he knew who I was. I explained to him what happened and that I did appreciate what she had asked me to do. He understood but at the same time I felt he was also making excuses for her knowing she was wrong. He agreed to speak to her regarding the matter. When things like this transpired it made me keep an eye on Jorgia even more. Everyone knew how I was with Jorgia, and some understood and then you had those that understood but still tried to get away with not doing what was needed. Regardless of whether they thought it necessary or not they had to follow a doctor's instructions for that child. There is no going around it and I was going to make sure it was followed correctly. I wasn't going anywhere so they just had to get used to it.

Jorgia tantrums subsided in the car due to the fact she was now on the bus and not in the car as much. I was still waiting on National Seating Mobility to measure her for a harness for the car that would protect me from her. She was able to get out of her seat belt but with the harnesses she would be secured in her seat. Until then I had to have her sit in the middle whenever she was in the car and crisscross her seat belt with all the seat belts in the back seat so she couldn't get to me to hurt or hit the windows. I hated doing this, but I think for her she felt more safe and secure that way. It actually looked worse than what it really was. I did notice when she was in the car she would mostly just scream and cry like something was bothering her. I just couldn't figure it out.

Within a couple of days Jorgia got up in the morning for school and went to the potty. I came into the bathroom to clean her when she leaned forward, I gasped with shock, as my hand covered my mouth. I saw a huge cyst right at the top crack of her butt. It was oozing and bleeding. I thought what the hell is going on now. This poor child can't catch a damn break. I had no idea what this was, how it got there, how long it had been there and what we were about to embark upon. All I could do was try and get her to a doctor immediately.

I got her dressed and headed straight to urgent care. I checked in and waited anxiously for the doctor. We didn't wait very long which was greatly appreciated. When I got into the room I sat there extremely worried about what this could be. I felt so bad for Jorgia. I wish it was me instead of her.

"God... hasn't she been through enough?," I thought. The doctor entered the room and had her lay on her belly to take a look at what was going on. He took a good look at it and then informed me that it was a Pilonidal Cyst, and he was going to have to lance the cyst to drain it. The doctor told me he didn't understand how she was functioning with this cyst. It was known to be very painful. He was surprised she could even sit down. This kid has had so many different things happen to her that I have never heard of. Her pain tolerance was unbelievable. I felt so bad she had to go through this right now. I hate the fact that she never knows what's about to happen to her. I hate the fact that she wasn't able to tell me she was in pain, I wanted to brace her for what was coming, but she wouldn't understand and that just crushed my soul.

I had to get her to lay on her belly as they prepped to cut the cyst open. He had to give her a few shots to numb the area. She never cried but she jerked so quickly it scared the shit out of me. Once the area was fully numb he began to cut the cyst open, I started to feel nauseous and wanted to pass out after seeing the pus and blood oozing from this cyst. It totally reminded me of Dr. Pimple Popper. After squeezing out much as he could and cleaning the area he packed it with the string gauze and bandaged up the area. He also called in some antibiotics to kill any infection before it got worse. I had to make sure I returned the next day to remove the gauze. Once the gauze was removed it had to remain uncovered and re-packed daily. I also had to give her warm sitz baths soaking the area hoping to drain anything else that needed to drain. When I wasn't able to do the baths I had to use warm face towels on the area 2 to 3 times a day. Giving her Ibuprofen every four hours helped manage her pain.

Over the next couple of weeks, I was doing all this and trying to protect the area from her. It started to look a little better and was starting to close up, but it still was somewhat inflamed. I was sending a pillow to school and to the autism center for her comfort. One morning she went to the potty as usual, when I came into the bathroom I noticed blood all over the back of the toilet. Because it was healing it started to itch so she was trying to find a little relief by scratching the area and accidentally scratched the incision open again.

I didn't like the way it was looking, and I was tired of dealing with this cyst. It was so stubborn. It just wouldn't fully go away fast enough. I called her doctor who thought she needed to see a surgeon. She wasted no time referring her over to a pediatric surgeon at Valley Children's Hospital. I had been at his hospital so much I felt as if I worked there. It became our second home. I called the surgeon's office and scheduled to bring her in. They wanted to see right away.

Before her appointment I had to have surgery on my right shoulder even though both shoulders had partial tears and bone spurs. Surgery had to be done on the right shoulder first. They believe it was wear and tear over the years taking care of Jorgia. She was a big girl that really couldn't do anything for herself. She didn't even start feeding herself until she was about eight years old due to her motor skills. I was still dressing her, tending to her bathroom duties, fighting her several times a day during her violent meltdowns. It had finally all caught up to me. My shoulder was in constant pain which is what led to the surgery.

I had to train my husband for the first time on everything he needed to do for Jorgia. He had to everything from taking her and picking her up from the center, packing her two backpacks with her lunches for school and the autism center, her medication, putting her to bed and dealing with her tantrums. Unfortunately, he had to take care of me too because I now had one arm and in a lot of pain. I was going to have to go to physical therapy twice a week starting two weeks after my surgery.

Once my surgery was done my husband was off work on PFL (Paid Family Leave) until I recovered. He was able to accompany me to the surgeon's office with Jorgia for her appointment. Since she couldn't walk long distances due to her Gait Dyspraxia we always used her wheelchair when taking her to appointments. We wheeled her up to the surgeon office and they were able to get us back rather quickly because of George's Law. She was already restless and ready to leave. We were trying to play with her and talk to her to keep her mind off wanting to leave. The doctor finally came into the room and asked us to get her onto the table onto her belly so she could see what's going on with this cyst. She removed the bandages and told us what we dreaded to hear. Jorgia was going to have to have surgery as soon as possible. They need to completely cut it open and clean it out down through her tail bone.

Autism, Cystic Fibrosis, Gait Dyspraxia, psoriasis, catching COVID and now this. God once again isn't this enough? Where are you God? Help her! Help me! Please, God I'm begging you! I wished I could go back in the past and fix whatever I did wrong to deserve the wrath of God because this was way too much for one person. Why did I bring her into this world just to be tortured. I didn't know how much more I could take. No matter how I felt, we had to get prepared for this surgery that had to be done. Before leaving the office we set the date for her surgery which would only be within a couple of days.

We arrived at the hospital very early in the morning. She didn't have anything to eat or drink. This brought back memories from her other surgery, so it wasn't all new. The doctor and anesthesiologist came in as expected to explain the procedure and how long it would take. We were just ready to get it over with. They gave her a little medication just like before to calm her before taking her back to the operating room. When we knew she was OK, we said our good-byes with kisses, hugs, and a lot of love. During moments like this, it didn't matter how I felt or what I had been through. All that mattered was that my baby girl would get through this and be OK. I was ready to get back to our normal…maybe not all of it!

The wait as usual was intense. We were nervous and very tired. A lot had been going on and we still had a bit of a hill to climb after this surgery, but we knew together we would get through it just fine. I couldn't help but worry that it was just the mom in me that would never change, especially when it came to my children and husband.

We decided to make a quick run to the store to get something to eat and some coffee along with some fresh air. It was hard just sitting there watching the clock. As soon as we were coming out of the store, my phone rang. It was the nurse telling us Jorgia was in recovery asking for us. We never moved so fast trying to get to our baby girl. Gary got us back as quickly as he could. We were so fortunate that her surgery went great. She was happy to see us when we walked in where she was resting peacefully. She was ready to go home and so were we.

The doctor explained they would be sending her home with a hole where the cyst was and that they couldn't close the hole because they had to allow it to heal from the inside out. We had to make sure we pulled the gauze out daily like before and re-pack it, then bandage the area so the drainage wouldn't get on her clothing. I was happy she was OK and excited to get home. I knew this would be a long process and it wasn't going to be easy, but nothing with or about Jorgia was ever easy. Over a few months it would heal, and she would end up reopening the wound a couple of times. I have to say we are still dealing with her cyst on and off today. Like I said before, it's Jorgia I wouldn't have expected it any other way.

Chapter 19

I know my life with Jorgia has been difficult in more ways than I can imagine. I can't express enough how much I love my daughter. Everything she has put me through was not her fault. Everything that had happened to her was unfortunate and so undeserved. I have talked about how Autism has ruined my life and took everything from me, which is still true. However, Autism ruined Jorgia's life as well. Autism stole her identity; Autism took away who she could have been and who she could have become.

I know at times I have said I hated Jorgia, but I realized I never hated her, I hated autism, and I hated what autism had done to our family. I hated that because of autism I had no control, Autism came into our lives and destroyed everything in its path. Autism was so demanding it left me feeling lost, confused, and exhausted. It literally sucked the life out of me, and it turned my daughter into a raging beast.

On the other side of this horrible experience, I came to understand that Jorgia being diagnosed with autism actually turned out to be a real gift. If it wasn't for her I wouldn't have never known how strong I could be. I wouldn't have never found out how much fight I had in me. It's true that I may have lost myself but the person I had become was a better version of myself. Jorgia empowered me, Jorgia motivated me to be better, to never give up, to want to help other people that were going through what I was going through. How could I have done that If I would have never been given the opportunity to face autism head on.

Things really do happen for a reason because I had learned so much from my baby girl. I thought I was teaching her, and she was the one actually teaching me. Seeing how strong Jorgia was and how much she endured drove me to keep going. There was nothing wrong with how I felt through the years, my feelings were valid. I needed to go through what I went through so I could come out on the other side more knowledgeable, more prepared, and ready to stand up and take on the world for Jorgia. Autism wasn't going to beat us, I couldn't let it continue to break us, I refused to let it take us down. There were times when it came very close, but I stood strong and now I have more control than I ever knew existed.

I still had moments that I was depressed, I still had bad days, but it was Jorgia that continued to be my reason to get up, she was so demanding I had no time to sit in self-pity. I'm human. I do have times where I cry myself to sleep, I have times I still want to give up, I even still pray God just take me in my sleep. These are my weakest moments, the ones that I can't help. I don't judge anyone anymore because of what I've been through. What someone is feeling you have to pay attention and believe them.

Autism isn't going anywhere as a matter of fact it is evolving and it's such a wide spectrum. Every child is different from mild, moderate, to severe, which doesn't matter at all. This monster we call "Autism" will affect or change our lives forever. There is no preparation, there is no getting ready, when it comes into your life it will come when least expected, and one with an unimaginable force. There is no instruction manual, there is no video, there is no cure or medication, there is nothing, but you and your child left alone to figure it all out.

When Jorgia was diagnosed, I was told about it and then sent home with no next steps. No one called from the psychologist office or doctor office to see if I was OK or needed anything. Sadly, it's not their job. Their job is to give you the results of the test and that's it. This breaks my heart and angers me that there's no support after being told something as devastating as your child has AUTISM. What are we supposed to do?

Where do we go? Who do we call? What do we expect? Will they be able to function normally? No one is around to answer those questions.

When I got back home after the diagnosis I had a little girl standing there that I wanted to help but had no clue how. She was looking to me for guidance and I didn't even have a location, not even a plan, I was in the dark on what autism was even about. I felt so bad for my daughter who did not choose to be in this world and now was faced with an unfamiliar obstacle that altered everything that was familiar. Jorgia didn't understand that the gift was her existence. I needed my daughter, and to me she was normal. It was a new normal that we had to adjust to.

My journey has been tough but when Jorgia has good days, it makes every day of the journey so worth it. When I come into the room and see her smiling, my heart turns to butter. I call her Miss Diva because she sits on the couch making demands all day. She makes me laugh when I see her scrolling on her tablet listening to music. She has always loved music. I think Jorgia would have made a great DJ. We are still trying to teach her to be a little more independent. She does OK when her good days are on, but when her bad days hit, that's a different story. I try to keep things simple with Jorgia. I know she doesn't like going out or being around a lot of people, so I try to avoid taking her places and we avoid crowds. With COVID a lot of that has calmed down anyway.

My husband Gary and I purchased a home back in 2015 and I couldn't wait to decorate her room. I made her room purple and orange with butterflies. I know with autism they didn't understand much but Jorgia understood a lot more than we gave her credit for. She loved the color purple, and I loved butterflies because of the meaning behind them. I knew Jorgia loved the color purple because she spent so much time in the children's hospital where their rooms were this beautiful purple color, it was sort of calming.

During one of her Cystic Fibrosis episodes when she was younger, my husband decided before she was released to come home he wanted to paint her room that same purple. We were always trying to implement things in our home that would calm her. Anything that helped we were always willing to try it. I even got her a purple see through bed canopy net that went over her bed, with colorful butterflies everywhere. It was a princess room made for a princess. When purchasing our home, I kept that same theme with more butterflies hanging from her ceiling and added the color orange to break up the purple. One of my loves was home decorating so it was my pleasure and honor to do this for my baby girl. I had to find a way to do things I loved to do as well. It was like finding pieces of myself in those moments. The butterflies for me were intriguing, how from a caterpillar it becomes a butterfly. This symbolized autism as the caterpillar which became my beautiful Jorgia who is my butterfly.

Even though things were put in a better perspective for me, autism was still definitely taking a toll on me. Being locked up with Jorgia for over a year because of COVID I really needed a break. My husband and I missed our anniversary because of it. I hadn't been able to get away just to recharge for a very long time. I wanted to get away from the chaos autism and COVID had brought into my home. Plus, I was at my breaking point which felt like I was drowning, and I needed a raft. I felt like my chest was caving in and I needed air. Going through these daily rages hurt so bad it felt like my heart was being ripped from my chest. I could never get used to this. I don't think Jorgia even recognized me when she emerged from her tantrums. My husband recognized how broken I was and wanted to get me away from it all at least for a few days.

We decided to go to Vegas for the weekend. He wanted to catch a flight because I had never been on a plane before. I thought that was a brilliant idea, I was over the moon excited. I couldn't sit down, I couldn't even sleep, I was so ready. I was nervous about the flight, but I was ready for something new, I was ready for a different experience other than the one I was trapped in.

We booked the flight; we booked the hotel room which was very beautiful. We also were elated to find out one of our favorite comedians Eddie Griffin was going to be there doing a show, so we had to get tickets. This was going to be one of the best weekends I have had in years. I was anxiously waiting for the day.

The day was vastly approaching, and we were days away from leaving. I got an email from the airline thinking it was our tickets. I opened the email and was devastated as I read that our flight was canceled, the reason was unknown. I was so disappointed. We tried everything in our power to find another flight, but we just couldn't make it happen and the prices went up on top of it all. I was stunned that this was happening. I had to take a deep breath and figure out what our options were because nothing was going to get in the way of me going. I needed this. I deserved this.

I knew getting away would help me not only recharge, but it would help me clear my mind and get some well needed rest so I could be in a better place and be a better version of myself for Jorgia. Dealing with her I needed all the strength I could get. I knew I would worry about her as I always do. I text constantly checking on her because I'm always afraid something is happening to her, or she will get sick and I'm not there. I would always stress myself out worrying about her. I was a mess. I wanted to get away but at the same time I didn't want to leave her. I was completely torn, but I knew I had to do this for my sanity.

We decided to drive to Vegas which would be a six-hour drive. I was disappointed about the flight, but I was still excited to get away and finally have some fun. My daughter Shana was watching Jorgia which put my mind at ease. I knew Shana as her sister knew how to care for her probably just as well as I did, so I knew she was in good hands. Having that trust with someone watching your child is very important and goes a long way. It relieved so much pressure and I appreciated her wholeheartedly because I know Jorgia is beyond hard work and I didn't take that lightly.

The day for our trip came, and I was feeling something that was so unfamiliar, I didn't recognize it. I hadn't had this feeling since forever. It was happiness, I had forgotten what that felt like and it was amazing. It was a great feeling to have something to look forward to. We hit the road anticipating that six-hour drive, but it also gave us a chance to talk and spend some quality time that was hard to do at home in the midst of the chaos we lived in. We did just that, I enjoyed every moment. I was taking it all in, I hung onto every word my husband was saying. We talked about everything, reminisced, and laughed so hard we cried. I was snapping pictures of the beautiful mountain scenery. It was absolutely gorgeous. It was incredible. We arrived in Vegas and right off the freeway was the massive brand-new Raiders Stadium. I had to get pictures of that as well. Even though I was enjoying myself like never before I was still checking up on Jorgia seeing how she was doing. I thought, am I crazy for missing her? No, I don't think I was, no matter what had happened she was still my daughter who I missed very much already. I was also used to things being a certain way for so long, my mind was still stuck there. It was difficult to take my thoughts in a different direction.

We arrived at the hotel to check in. There were crowds of people all around, slot machines were ringing, people were yelling and screaming, it was music to my ears. It was such a wonderful feeling to feel alive again. I was indebted to my husband for planning this unforgettable trip, for just thinking about me and understanding what I needed, as he always does. We headed to our room after checking in, dropped off our belongings and went down to the casino to play some slots and get a drink. I couldn't move fast enough. I was still checking in on Jorgia every chance I got. I wasn't surprised that she was doing very well, knowing she was OK I allowed myself to just let go and have fun.

I wanted to see and do everything. I didn't even want to blink because I was afraid I would miss something. The excitement was overwhelming. We hit the ground running, playing, drinking, winning, and losing. We were having the time of our lives. We headed outside as night began to fall to sight see a little, taking pictures and following the crowds to other casinos. A couple of hours later while we were sitting at some slot machines playing, I felt a dull pain on the right side of my abdomen that traveled around to my back. It almost felt like the same pain when I got really sick a year prior and found out I had gall stones and an infection and my gallbladder and had to have it removed. Since my gallbladder was gone I know it wasn't that, so I tried to ignore it. I started thinking maybe I was hungry, maybe it was gas, but whatever it was I figured it would just go away.

I kept playing, I kept drinking, but I was very uncomfortable. It was getting to the point I could hardly stand up straight. I told my husband maybe we should try to get something to eat. We found a restaurant and sat down as the pain was still nagging me profusely, but we still placed our order. There were so many people in there, there wasn't an empty seat in sight. While waiting on our food I was trying to ignore the pain that was slowly intensifying. I tried unbuttoning my pants, I tried drinking water, nothing was working. I was frustrated and confused because I never felt this before.

Our food arrived and I began eating. I took two bites, and the pain went from 50 to 100 within seconds. I told my husband we had to leave. I needed to lay down immediately. We asked for some take home containers figuring I would eat later once I started to feel better. I barely could walk, and I definitely wasn't able to stand up straight. My husband was holding me up trying to help me get back to the room. I laid on the bed in agonizing pain that just wouldn't stop. I tried taking pain medication, I tried going to the bathroom, I was trying everything, and nothing was helping. I was crying and moaning, I was so miserable. The pain continued all night, it was excruciating. I was confused because I had no idea what was going on with my body.

I slept on and off all night, but the pain never went away. I was so pissed off that I was going through this right now. At some point I managed to fall asleep for a few hours. When I woke up I could see the sunrise coming through the window. As I tried to sit up the pain was still there but not as bad.

I had a little bit of an appetite, so my husband ordered some fruit, crackers, and juice, just something to get me going. I was able to eat the fruit and drink some fluids. I felt so bad for my husband, I felt like I ruined the trip. He was so positive as usual, telling me it was not my fault. He sat at the desk and got some work done with his job as I continued to lay there trying to feel better. Later I told him I wanted to try going down to the casino. I needed to try and move around because I knew we still had the comedy show to go to later that evening. I didn't want to let on how horrible I actually felt but I'm sure he was aware of it. He said I looked pale. I was able to get up enough strength to get dressed and walk down to the casino. I wanted him to enjoy himself as much as possible. I didn't want to hold him back. This was an opportunity we may not get again for a long time. I wanted him to take full advantage.

We sat down at a couple of slots, and I was still feeling that pain so I just kind of laid on the machine with my head resting on my arm, watching my husband play. I wanted to join him, but I just didn't have the strength. We then decided to go outside to get some air and walk wanting to capture as much as possible while we were there. It was killing me that I was sick, I was heartbroken that the one chance I had to have a good time was panning out this way. We stopped in front of the beautiful waterfall and glamour hotels taking photos. You can plainly see in the pictures I was pale as my husband said. I looked sick for sure.

That evening it came time for the comedy show so we headed over to the spot. We stopped at the Noodle Bar to grab some of their famous chicken noodle soup hoping that would help with the pain that was still lingering. After we ate we went inside the comedy show where the lights were flashing, music was playing. It was definitely exciting, but I just couldn't fully be engaged. I totally felt out of it. I must admit I was ready to go home, only because of how I was feeling. Although I wasn't ready for what was waiting for me at home.

The comedy show began, and I was enjoying myself, having a few laughs and next thing I knew the show was over. I guess I had laid my head over on my husband's shoulder and fell asleep. I was embarrassed and I felt as if I let my husband down greatly. He managed to plan this trip for me, and this is how it went. What a disgrace! I was disappointed in myself even though I knew I couldn't help it. I was still emotionally distraught. We went back to the hotel and decided to turn in for the evening. I woke up the next morning, which was time to go home. I felt so much better, the pain was completely gone. I just couldn't believe it was gone the day it was time to return home. The drive home was devastating. I felt like nothing was accomplished and now it was back to reality still on a dead battery. I never got to recharge. I wasn't sure how much longer I could continue taking care of Jorgia running on literally nothing.

I know I would always think God hated me or was trying to punish me for my past. I now understand God was always preparing me for what was to come. He wanted me to see just how strong I really am, he knew I would be OK because he never left my side. I had to work harder than the next person at everything I wanted, nothing ever came easy. I felt like God's reasoning was to make us appreciate what we had. I was learning to stop complaining about what I did have or what I couldn't do and start appreciating what I did have and what I could do. My mom used to always tell me "There is always someone out there worse off than you." I didn't understand what that meant but now I get it.

I know everyone has a story and I never want to come off insensitive to anyone or what they were going through. I know my situation was not the worst, but the magnitude of what I was experiencing was very hard to accept. When you're in that moment everything you know goes out the window. It's hard to think clearly when your daughter slaps you so hard your glasses fly off, When your daughter bites you and leave an everlasting mark, when your daughter scratches you until your bleeding, when your daughter is destroying your home and you can't get her under control, when your dodging things being thrown at you from every direction, when your ears are ringing from disturbing screams and stretching sounds you've never heard in your life. There's no way to think clearly, it's even hard to be positive. The only thing I could do is cry, I cried so much that the migraines became part of my day.

I hated when people who had no children or didn't have any children with disabilities would try to give me advice on what I should try to do or how I should feel. I wanted to tell them to please shut up! They seriously had no idea, and this made me so angry. They couldn't even begin to understand my situation and I didn't want them to. I just wanted to vent, I just wanted support, I just wanted them to understand where I was coming from.

When my husband was helping me after my shoulder surgery when he was the front runner on caring for Jorgia I remember him telling me how he had a newfound respect for what I did on a daily basis. He said he always knew what I was going through but now that he was the one that had to take the reins. He said now he REALLY knew what I was going through, and he was so much more empathetic to my situation.

Chapter 20

Autism is no joke. I had gathered so much information over the years and wanted to disperse everything I knew to help anyone I could. I know everyone may have a different journey or a different story, but I was here to tell my experiences to hopefully help someone the way I wanted to be helped. I want parents like me to know they are not alone. I don't want them to have half-truths, I don't want them to go into this blind or think it's no big deal, I want them to know their feelings matter and how they feel is valid.

This autism journey for me has been the most difficult thing that has ever happened to me. It disrupted my life that I thought I had planned out perfectly. I wasn't ready or equipped for this life altering diagnosis. I want to be as truthful and transparent as possible. If I had a choice when they tested me when I was pregnant with Jorgia for mental retardation or any other health issues and if it would of came back positive, showing autism or cystic fibrosis I probably would have had an abortion. Don't get me wrong I love my daughter but my reasoning for saying that is because I wouldn't have wanted this for her.

This was not something I would choose, and I don't think anyone else would have chosen to live with autism or any other disability if they had the opportunity to say yes or no. As I have said many times I love my daughter and wouldn't trade her for anything now but looking back on what I have gone through and still have a whole journey in front of me I wouldn't take it on if I had that choice.

My daughter is 14 now and in high school, we have come a long way. Now at 14 try to understand Jorgia is as tall as me, if not taller, she is stronger than you can imagine weighing about 145 pounds, her screams are disturbing and can't be duplicated. I can hardly handle her when she is in full tantrum mode. She swings at me like we are in a boxing rink. I, on the other hand, am now 50 years old with several health issues. I'm not as strong as I used to by any means. I have arthritis as well, my bones ache constantly and my muscles are always sore. I still need one more shoulder surgery that I may have to pass on. I'm extremely sleep deprived and so exhausted I can hardly stay awake on most days. This is why I am still considering a home for her, maybe when she turns 18. It is still a discussion between my husband and me. It's still not for certain but definitely an option and a lot of things to consider. It's not an easy decision but it is a big decision, and we will always do what's best for Jorgia she is number one.

It is unknown what will happen or where we will be health wise and where she will be far as her behavior overall. I just know I'm not getting any younger and I have to start planning for the future. It tears me apart to even have to consider this option. I want her with me until the end of time, but I'm so unsure if I will be able to control her tantrums and be able to prevent her from harming herself or others too. It was a sad harsh reality that I really didn't like to talk about, but we had to at least discuss it from time to time. It would have to be a decision we would have to make together; Jorgia isn't just my daughter. Her father Gary loves her just as much as I do, if not more. He adores Jorgia. He calls her Coop or Coopy and she loves it, and she loves her Da Da. They have a special unbreakable bond. Jorgia also loves her siblings. She hangs out with her brothers and learns all the latest music or rap songs on the radio and then plays them on her tablet. They would take photos with her and video's, she just loved the attention. They never treated her like she had autism. She was so smart that she has them eating out of the palm of her hand. She is so spoiled, and she knows it.

She totally surprises me when she asks for something like juice, and I tell her no then she asks her dad. The typical child or teenager goes to the other parent when the other one says no. I enjoy these moments with Jorgia. There are not very many, but I definitely cherish them when they happen. Knowing there was a time we didn't think we would ever see her doing things like this or even ever hear her voice, it was a true blessing to witness her progression.

I had someone say to me just put her in a group home, and I was speechless. It's not that easy at least for me and how awful for anyone to make such a suggestion for someone else's child, especially one that has a disability. Some people unfortunately are very selfish, inconsiderate, and just plain old ignorant. This was my baby and whether she has Autism or not you don't just throw away your child. Children that don't have Autism or a disability do things to get on our nerves or cause problems and we don't just give them away. Having autism doesn't make you less human, autism doesn't make them less your child or give you the right to give up on them. We are all they have, we are their voice, we have to get to know them in their own little world.

Autism has been a blessing and a curse. It might sound strange, but I wouldn't be where I am today if it wasn't for Jorgia having autism. I would not have been able to help the people that have reached out to me for information or advice. Autism has opened my eyes to things I was blind to. I see the world from a whole new set of eyes and now have a different perspective on all disabilities. Autism is not just a disability it gives us an ability to be taught, the ability to help others, the ability to understand the misunderstood, the ability to change who we are for the better, the ability to dig deep within ourselves and find a strength we never knew existed. For me most of all Autism gave me the ability to see Jorgia as a real gift from God.

I questioned God so much, wanting to always know why. Praying he would work a miracle, going through depression and the whole time all the answers were right there in front of me. God has always been here guiding me. I had to slow down and just listen and take in what I was being shown. I was so focused on all the negatives it was hard to see the positives. Autism doesn't just go away and I'm still learning every day. Jorgia will be this way the rest of her life and I have learned to accept that. It's not a bad thing. I can still have dreams and hopes, I can still do things I love to do, I can still have a prosperous life. I just had to start making Some adjustments, start planning things around her and stop forcing things on her.

It's OK to cry, you will have bad days, she will still have tantrums and all that stuff she has done, it doesn't go away if anything it will get worse because she is older and smarter. You have to come to grips with it and know that it's still OK. You take one day at a time. You can still have those deep dark moments, it doesn't make you a bad person or a bad mom, it makes you human. Autism alone will cause you to fall, but you get back up, you figure it out and you make the best of what you were given. It took me years to develop this state of mind. I thought I was going to go insane. I never thought I would be where I am with autism now. Autism has motivated me even more to make sure Jorgia voice is heard. Just because she has autism doesn't mean she doesn't deserve the best. She wants to be loved like anyone else, she wants attention like anyone else, she wants to be held like anyone else, she wants to be seen or noticed like anyone else, she wants to be like everyone else.

Before Jorgia was born Autism was just another word. I heard of it but didn't know anything about autism. I was not as empathetic to people with disabilities as I should have been. It wasn't that I ignored disabled people or was mean to them, I just didn't see them or notice them. The way I do now. Through the eyes of autism. Now they are the first ones I notice. If Jorgia is with me or we are out in public I can see or feel people looking at me the way I used to look at them. I felt unseen, I felt ignored, and no one was paying me any attention. They noticed me but they didn't see me. If she is acting out they just starred. They don't mean any harm they just don't understand, they have no clue what your journey is about. I used to be like them until autism woke me up and gave me the opportunity to experience my own journey to hopefully change the world one person at a time.

I didn't choose autism, autism chose us. God trusted me to handle his angle, this beautiful special gift with care. I was confused in the beginning on what I was supposed to do, I was afraid because I wasn't aware of what the future held for me or Jorgia. I fought against autism for so long and it was winning. Once I was able to begin understanding it more, I began figuring out how to not feed what made autism angry. I learned how to stay calm because autism would react even worse when it was feeding off your emotions. I didn't always have the answers, but we were starting to have more good days than bad and that was more than what I could ask for. All the little things counted; the big accomplishments were a bonus.

It was rare that Jorgia was quiet. Don't get me wrong I enjoyed it but sometimes the quietness scared me. It was like the calm before the storm. The hardest part was I just couldn't let my guard down, I couldn't relax, not even for a minute. As soon as I think she is good, everything is going so well, a storm would hit all of a sudden destroying everything in its path. Autism was very brutal and left you completely empty and overwhelming.

Her therapist at CARD taught me how important it was for me to learn from every single experience, what was happening before she got upset that could have triggered her. I learned to try to do things to detour the behavior, keep her busy before the meltdowns have a chance to cause her to explode. I began to use timers for waiting because most children with autism are very visual. These were just a few things that became pivotal moments during this journey. Even when I'm driving it was important to use visuals for her to see where we were going, removing each destination once we reached it. These were all very helpful but not always.

I didn't expect it to be perfect or these things to cure autism. I just wanted to tame the beast that was making life impossible to live. I wanted to take back control and that was by doing all the small things that would get better and better each time. I was striving for peace, and I knew it would take hard work and I was willing to do what I had to do to get there. If I made it this far without the tools I needed I knew with the tools I have now I was about to become a force to be reckoned with against autism. I learned to get out of my head, I learned to get out of self. All this time I was stuck on how I was feeling and what I was experiencing, what I lost, and I had that right. I didn't know any other way to feel because I was trapped in the diagnosis not to mention how lost I was in the devastation of autism. But now I was more tuned into how Jorgia felt, what she was experiencing, how scared she must of felt, how confused she was. It was all about her, she was the one autism had taken control of. I was always fighting against Jorgia without realizing it, but now I wanted to fight for her the right way and fight with her. It was me and her against autism. I had been able to make some things happen from standing my ground with her. Jorgia was stubborn, but I wouldn't cave most of the time. The mom in me did give in some of the time. When she was younger I knew how to fight but now I have learned to direct my energy more on gaining better control of Jorgia so we can bring peace back into our home.

My main goal was to help other moms however I could and to be there for them in any way. I wanted them to know they are not alone. I know how scary this could be and we were in this together. I wanted them to realize what a gift autism was. I wanted to teach them how to look at things from another perspective. Trying to see the world from their child's eyes would help understand them better. I wanted them to know how to take back the power early don't wait so late like I did.

Don't ever let anyone tell you nothing is wrong with your child if your motherly intuition is telling you something is different. Trust your instincts, no one knows your child the way you do. Never give up, your child is counting on you to get it right. They are waiting on you to help them, they are waiting on your guidance. I know it's a lot of pressure and a massive amount of work, but your child has no one else to depend on.

I also learned to not take Jorgia attacking me so personally. Now, this was a really hard one. I broke down every time because I wanted to feel loved by Jorgia and she would treat me so awful, but she had no idea what she was doing or how she was making me feel.

What was difficult was having four children before Jorgia. I could discipline them when they did something wrong or was disrespectful. I could put them on punishment, I could put them in time out, I could take things away from them making them earn them back. I was able to have control as a mother should. With autism I had to surrender that control to autism, because there was no way to discipline Jorgia the way I disciplined them. I could punish her to a certain extent. We tried things like five-minute time outs which seemed to piss her off even more.

Attending CARD was even challenging for the staff. Jorgia had so many different programs to work on they always had to put their best experienced therapist or her case. Jorgia was a special case; she was a hard nut to crack and very stubborn. As soon as you think you have her figured out or think you're making progress she proves you wrong then it's back to the drawing board. Just as Jorgia would challenge me she was also challenging them, because with Jorgia she was having issues they had never faced before. They never would give up though, and they were always willing to do whatever it takes to help me with my daughter. Their goal was to help make my life easier as much as possible. The team is made up of trained professionals in this field and know what it takes. I was soaking up any information they could give me. They all loved Jorgia, and everyone enjoyed working with her. It made me feel good to know she was in good hands with people that truly cared about her. There was no greater feeling than being able to trust someone fully with your child, especially one with a disability.

One of my worst fears was leaving Jorgia with someone that treated her bad and she wouldn't be able to tell me. I never wanted to find out what I was capable of if I ever found out someone messed with my daughter. She was my heart, and I would do anything I had to do to protect her. I was irritated and annoyed at the stories I would hear on the news and the internet about parents of all people abusing their kids that had autism, the ones that are supposed to protect them. Why? How could they do this? I was confused. I was so angry it made me want to hold my daughter even tighter. There was one article I read that a mother had her son's vocal cords removed because she couldn't stand the screams. This was beyond insane! What doctor would even sign off on this. These are things that made me want to stand up and fight for these kids. I knew God wanted me to do my job and I wasn't going to stop until it was done.

The things I would hear about teachers abusing autistic students, and the actions caught on camera fueled the fire burning inside me for these helpless kids that couldn't help what was happening to them. These children could not defend themselves and most of all they did not ask to be born, period. The stuff I would read broke my heart. I had to stop watching the news and stay off the internet because I felt helpless. All I could do is give Jorgia everything I had hoping to inspire other parents to want more for their children. I wanted to be their example that it could be done.

Why was it so hard to love these kids? Now I am questioning God again, why would you give these parents these special gifts only for them to turn around and hurt or abused them? They didn't deserve such a gift. So again, did God make a mistake? These kids being abused was happening more often than usual. I finally figured it out. After what I had been through with Jorgia, I understood why these parents and other

people were abusing these kids. They had no idea how to deal with something as difficult as Autism. We were being sent home once given the diagnosis to figure it out on our own. Everyone isn't like me, willing to put in the work to research. So, when this child is having tantrums or meltdowns they let their emotions take over and get physical with a child that can't defend themselves. They didn't understand autism at all. They just took it as that child being defiant and didn't know how to set aside their anger. These parents didn't know how to take their feelings out of it because the child could not control their actions. If they would have taken the time to research, ask questions, or ask for help then maybe that would have saved a child from being abused or even killed.

Psychologists should come up with a way to send the parents of these children home with them knowing someone would follow up with them to offer help or answer questions. Parents need someone that can assist them in any way for a period of time. This would really help take a load off the parent's mind. There is no way they could go home with a clear mind after receiving such devastating news.

I'm on a mission for Jorgia and all the children out there with disabilities, especially kids with autism. Teachers need special training; they need patience with these special children. It is not called special needs for nothing. I am so passionate because of my daughter, that's why I always stay very close to her. I know who her teachers are and communicate with them constantly through the day for everything. They are very good at messaging me back very quickly, because they know how I am about Jorgia. I want to know what she eats. How much did she eat that day? Did she have a bowel movement? How is acting? I have to know what state of mind my

daughter is in at all times. I need to know these things so I'll know will she be hungry when she gets home? Asking about the bowel movements helps me to know if she constipated. We have to keep up with our children. I am not joking when I say I had to become Jorgia, I really did. That was the only way to really understand the dynamic of autism. Even when they are hospitalized, know who their doctors are, who the nurses are, what meds they are giving them. Question everything and don't stop until you are satisfied with the answer.

Jorgia and I have a bright future ahead of us. I am certain the fight will never end. I am determined to advocate for our voiceless children. Autistic children have a lot to say but will never be able to say it. Jorgia is definitely coming along, speaking very little but for the most part she knows how to ask for what she wants. Sometimes it's not clear, and it takes a few times asking her to repeat herself until I finally understand what she is asking for. Jorgia is not quite self-sufficient yet, it's definitely a work in progress, but I'm very hopeful. She still is unable to dress or undress herself. She definitely still has uncontrollable tantrums and extreme meltdown. We are doing our best to get in front of them but still have a lot to figure out. She is 14 years old and in high school, it's unreal how time flies, but she is still a baby to me, my baby.

She is potty trained with occasional accidents which is expected, so she does still wear pull-ups only to bed every night. Being that she is bigger now, her pee has doubled making it onto her sheets, it's a lot. We are also still dealing with this cyst on her back that may require another surgery. If she does I will be there every step of the way.

I wish this little girl knew how special she is to me and how much I want the best for her. I wish she only knew if I could trade places with her I would in a heartbeat. I wish she knew mom will always fight for her and will never give up. I hope she knows how much I love her even through all the attacks. I wish she only knew how much she changed my life for the better. It took some time to see and understand that but now I understand this is what I'm supposed to be doing. I needed this wake-up call. If things would have been easy for me I would have never known what it was like to work hard for what you want, and it also makes you appreciate when you accomplish what you were working towards. Nothing in my life has ever come easy and I'm stronger because of it. God knew exactly what he was doing when he allowed them to place my autistic child in my arms. Only he knew what I was in for, and he never left my side, he trusted me with his most precious angel, and I won't let him down. I thank God now every day for this gift called Jorgia. September 3, 2008 was the day I gave birth to my angel and the day I was reborn as well. It's because of her that I am who I am today.

She taught me to trust myself, she taught me to go for what I want, she taught me how important it is to help people. You never know how you can affect someone else's life when you help them. She made me realize that I am good enough. She taught me to stop worrying about what other people thought, because of her I have learned to never take things for granted even the small things in life we think means nothing. She taught me it's OK to be mad, it's OK to feel angry, that my feelings matter, she taught me to trust my instincts because everyone doesn't always have the right intentions. We always search for things in our lives to fill some sort of emptiness but one time the very thing we are searching for most of the time is right in front of us. I thought that I wanted all these things in life, but I didn't need any of that stuff. What we need and what we want are 2 different things. What I needed was always right there, Jorgia was everything I needed and wanted, she is an amazing girl, and I am honored to be her mom. I will spend the rest of my life making sure she can be all she can be. I brought her into this world and autism has tried to ruin our lives but instead it enhanced our lives in more ways I can describe. It's true that we actually turned a curse into a blessing.

However, I am proud of myself and especially proud of Jorgia, she had been through so much and little did she know she was my hero, my inspiration, my strength that I need to move on in my life. I thought I missed out on becoming a singer, not being able to travel, not becoming an artist, or becoming an interior decorator. All these things I wanted out of life meant nothing to me and was not meant to be. I was meant to be a wife, a mother and most of all I was meant to be the mother of Jorgia who is the real gift inside autism... and our journey continues.